Gaming Programs for All Ages at the Library

PRACTICAL GUIDES FOR LIBRARIANS

About the Series

This innovative series written and edited for librarians by librarians provides authoritative, practical information and guidance on a wide spectrum of library processes and operations.

Books in the series are focused, describing practical and innovative solutions to a problem facing today's librarian and delivering step-by-step guidance for planning, creating, implementing, managing, and evaluating a wide range of services and programs.

The books are aimed at beginning and intermediate librarians needing basic instruction/guidance in a specific subject and at experienced librarians who need to gain knowledge in a new area or guidance in implementing a new program/service.

About the Series Editors

The **Practical Guides for Librarians** series was conceived and edited by M. Sandra Wood, MLS, MBA, AHIP, FMLA, Librarian Emerita, Penn State University Libraries from 2014-2017.

M. Sandra Wood was a librarian at the George T. Harrell Library, the Milton S. Hershey Medical Center, College of Medicine, Pennsylvania State University, Hershey, PA, for over thirty-five years, specializing in reference, educational, and database services. Ms. Wood received an MLS from Indiana University and an MBA from the University of Maryland. She is a fellow of the Medical Library Association and served as a member of MLA's Board of Directors from 1991 to 1995.

Ellyssa Kroski assumed editorial responsibilities for the series beginning in 2017. She is the director of Information Technology at the New York Law Institute as well as an award-winning editor and author of 36 books including *Law Librarianship in the Digital Age* for which she won the AALL's 2014 Joseph L. Andrews Legal Literature Award. Her ten-book technology series, *The Tech Set* won the ALA's Best Book in Library Literature Award in 2011. Ms. Kroski is a librarian, an adjunct faculty member at Drexel and San Jose State University, and an international conference speaker. She has just been named the winner of the 2017 Library Hi Tech Award from the ALA/LITA for her long-term contributions in the area of Library and Information Science technology and its application.

Titles in the Series edited by M. Sandra Wood

1. *How to Teach: A Practical Guide for Librarians* by Beverley E. Crane
2. *Implementing an Inclusive Staffing Model for Today's Reference Services* by Julia K. Nims, Paula Storm, and Robert Stevens

3. *Managing Digital Audiovisual Resources: A Practical Guide for Librarians* by Matthew C. Mariner
4. *Outsourcing Technology: A Practical Guide* ⸻ ⸻ by Robin Hastings
5. *Making the Library Accessible for All: A P* ⸻ ⸻ ⸻ Vincent
6. *Discovering and Using Historical Geograp* ⸻ ⸻ *al Guide for Librarians* by Eva H. Dodsworth and ⸻

7. *Digitization and Digital Archiving: A ⸻* Elizabeth R. Leggett
8. *Makerspaces: A Practical Guide for Librarians* by John J. Burke
9. *Implementing Web-Scale Discovery Services: A Practical Guide for Librarians* by JoLinda Thompson
10. *Using iPhones and iPads: A Practical Guide for Librarians* by Matthew Connolly and Tony Cosgrave
11. *Usability Testing: A Practical Guide for Librarians* by Rebecca Blakiston
12. *Mobile Devices: A Practical Guide for Librarians* by Ben Rawlins
13. *Going Beyond Loaning Books to Loaning Technologies: A Practical Guide for Librarians* by Janelle Sander, Lori S. Mestre, and Eric Kurt
14. *Children's Services Today: A Practical Guide for Librarians* by Jeanette Larson
15. *Genealogy: A Practical Guide for Librarians* by Katherine Pennavaria
16. *Collection Evaluation in Academic Libraries: A Practical Guide for Librarians* by Karen C. Kohn
17. *Creating Online Tutorials: A Practical Guide for Librarians* by Hannah Gascho Rempel and Maribeth Slebodnik
18. *Using Google Earth in Libraries: A Practical Guide for Librarians* by Eva Dodsworth and Andrew Nicholson
19. *Integrating the Web into Everyday Library Services: A Practical Guide for Librarians* by Elizabeth R. Leggett
20. *Infographics: A Practical Guide for Librarians* by Beverley E. Crane
21. *Meeting Community Needs: A Practical Guide for Librarians* by Pamela H. MacKellar
22. *3D Printing: A Practical Guide for Librarians* by Sara Russell Gonzalez and Denise Beaubien Bennett
23. *Patron-Driven Acquisitions in Academic and Special Libraries: A Practical Guide for Librarians* by Steven Carrico, Michelle Leonard, and Erin Gallagher
24. *Collaborative Grant-Seeking: A Practical Guide for Librarians* by Bess G. de Farber
25. *Story-Time Success: A Practical Guide for Librarians* by Katie Fitzgerald
26. *Teaching Google Scholar: A Practical Guide for Librarians* by Paige Alfonzo
27. *Teen Services Today: A Practical Guide for Librarians* by Sara K. Joiner and Geri Swanzy
28. *Data Management: A Practical Guide for Librarians* by Margaret E. Henderson
29. *Online Teaching and Learning: A Practical Guide for Librarians* by Beverley E. Crane
30. *Writing Effectively in Print and on the Web: A Practical Guide for Librarians* by Rebecca Blakiston
31. *Gamification: A Practical Guide for Librarians* by Elizabeth McMunn-Tetangco
32. *Providing Reference Services: A Practical Guide for Librarians* by John Gottfried and Katherine Pennavaria
33. *Video Marketing for Libraries: A Practical Guide for Librarians* by Heather A. Dalal, Robin O'Hanlan, and Karen Yacobucci

34. *Understanding How Students Develop: A Practical Guide for Librarians* by Hanah Gascho Rempel, Laurie M. Bridges, and Kelly McElroy
35. *How to Teach: A Practical Guide for Librarians, Second Edition* by Beverley E. Crane
36. *Managing and Improving Electronic Thesis and Dissertation Programs: A Practical Guide for Librarians* by Matthew C. Mariner
37. *User Privacy: A Practical Guide for Librarians* by Matthew Connolly
38. *Makerspaces: A Practical Guide for Librarians, Second Edition* by John J. Burke, revised by Ellyssa Kroski
39. *Summer Reading Programs for All Ages: A Practical Guide for Librarians* by Katie Fitzgerald
40. *Implementing the Information Literacy Framework: A Practical Guide for Librarians* by Dave Harmeyer and Janice J. Baskin

Titles in the Series edited by Ellyssa Kroski

41. *Finding and Using U.S. Government Information: A Practical Guide for Librarians* by Bethany Latham
42. *Instructional Design Essentials: A Practical Guide for Librarians* by Sean Cordes
43. *Making Library Web Sites Accessible: A Practical Guide for Librarians* by Laura Francabandera
44. *Serving LGBTQ Teens: A Practical Guide for Librarians* by Lisa Houde
45. *Coding Programs for Children and Young Adults in Libraries: A Practical Guide for Librarians* by Wendy Harrop
46. *Teen Fandom and Geek Programming: A Practical Guide for Librarians* by Carrie Rogers-Whitehead
47. *Comic Book Collections and Programming: A Practical Guide for Librarians* by Matthew Wood
48. *STEM Programming for All Ages: A Practical Guide for Librarians* by Chantale Pard

Titles in the Series edited by M. Sandra Wood

49. *Game-Based Teaching and Learning: A Practical Guide for Librarians* by Beverley E. Crane

Titles in the Series edited by Ellyssa Kroski

50. *Gaming Programs for All Ages at the Library: A Practical Guide for Librarians* by Tom Bruno

Gaming Programs for All Ages at the Library

A Practical Guide for Librarians

Tom Bruno

PRACTICAL GUIDES FOR LIBRARIANS, NO. 50

ROWMAN & LITTLEFIELD
Lanham • Boulder • New York • London

Published by Rowman & Littlefield
An imprint of The Rowman & Littlefield Publishing Group, Inc.
4501 Forbes Boulevard, Suite 200, Lanham, Maryland 20706
www.rowman.com

Unit A, Whitacre Mews, 26-34 Stannary Street, London SE11 4AB

British Library Cataloguing in Publication Information Available

Library of Congress Cataloging-in-Publication Data Available

ISBN 9781538108208 (pbk. : alk. paper) | ISBN 9781538108215 (electronic)

♾™ The paper used in this publication meets the minimum requirements of American National Standard for Information Sciences—Permanence of Paper for Printed Library Materials, ANSI/NISO Z39.48-1992.

Printed in the United States of America

Contents

Preface: My Own Personal Gaming Adventure   ix

Acknowledgments   xvii

CHAPTER 1. **A Short History and Survey of Gaming in
            Libraries**   1

CHAPTER 2. **Making Your Case for Library Gaming
            Programming with Stakeholders**   11

CHAPTER 3. **How to Acquire Games and Gaming
            Materials for Your Library with
            Minimal Overhead Cost**   19

CHAPTER 4. **How to Circulate Your Library Gaming
            Collection and Live to Tell the Tale**   25

CHAPTER 5. **How to Create, Evaluate, and Assess
            Gaming Programming for Your Library**   33

CHAPTER 6. **How to Implement Board Game
            Programming in Your Library**   41

CHAPTER 7. **How to Implement Video Game
            Programming in Your Library**   55

CHAPTER 8. **How to Support Pokémon GO and Other
            Augmented Reality Games at Your Library**   67

CHAPTER 9. **Role-Playing Games in the Library**   75

CHAPTER 10. **How to Run a Library Trivia Event**   95

CHAPTER 11. **How to Leverage Your MakerSpace to Help Bolster Your Library Gaming Program**   113

Bibliography: Leveling Up: Reading and Recommended Playing   127

Index   131

About the Author   135

Preface

My Own Personal Gaming Adventure

My story begins somewhere in the past. I was a newly minted librarian, just having completed my degree a year and half ago and only a few months into my first professional library position. The American Library Association was having its annual midwinter meeting in Philadelphia, Pennsylvania, which was as luck would have it close to my childhood home in South Jersey, so in between conference sessions, meeting with colleagues, and spending hours wandering the vast vending room floor, I also made plans to catch up with old friends from elementary and high school. One of my oldest friends was an automotive engineer who had a penchant for collecting old board games, and when I visited him during that weekend in January, he brought out what is considered to be one of the rarest and most beloved of 1980s board games: Milton Bradley's 1986 cult classic Fireball Island.

The rules of the game are rather simple—each player rolls a six-sided die and moves their little adventurer token the indicated number of spaces around the three-dimensional map of a mysterious island in search of a gem at the peak of the island's lone volcano, which is home to the volcano god Vul-Kar (naturally)—but the real fun happens whenever a player rolls a "1" on their die roll, unleashing the nominal fireballs after which the island and the game are so infamously named. The fireballs cascade down the nooks and crevices of the injection-molded game board seemingly with a mind of their own, adding a delightfully wicked element of chance and silliness to the game, and given that there is literally a one-in-six possibility of any player rolling a fireball on their turn, there are usually many reversals of fortune before one player ultimately wins the game by holding onto the gem and escaping the island and the other players to the safety of the mainland. While it's not exactly chess, Fireball Island adds a bit of strategy by including a deck of action cards that can be used to aid oneself or harm other players, so that even when the fireballs aren't taking out your opponents left and right, there are alternate ways to make them suffer.

My son, Mario, discovers the classic '80s board game Fireball Island.

I'm not sure if I ever actually played Fireball Island back in the 1980s, but I do remember that time period as being a golden era for similarly thematic board games with myriad hard-to-replace components: Scotland Yard, HeroQuest, Labyrinth, and Axis and Allies (which was itself a gateway game to war gaming), just to name a few. Still other games, such as Dark Tower and Stop Thief, even had sophisticated electronic components that helped randomize events without requiring a human antagonist or referee and speed up gameplay significantly. While board gaming had not yet become its own specialized kind of hobby, as it would around the turn of the twenty-first century, these initial forays into gaming were memorable insofar as they attempted to break out from the stereotypical restraints of the board games that had preceded them, such as Risk, Monopoly, or Clue. At any rate, after playing a couple of rounds of Fireball Island that night, I knew I was hooked on the game; and little did I know it at the time, but my reacquaintance with this cult classic would lead to an obsession with bringing this game to my library to share with old generations and new alike, providing a foundation for a robust library gaming program and ultimately leading to the writing of this book.

It probably goes without saying that I have always been a gamer. Growing up, I played any board game I could get my hands on, and although I never owned Fireball Island as a kid, I had several of the iconic games from the 1980s. Milton Bradley's Dark Tower (1981) was particularly appealing to me, as it was an epic fantasy quest that transformed its eponymous landmark into the computerized brains of the game. This molding of technology and board gaming that blends physical gaming with elements of computer, console, and arcade gaming will return as a theme time and time again in the history of gaming, with smartphones and tablets and specialized apps ultimately taking the place of dedicated electronic components. Dark Tower is also a great example of the intersection of board games with role-playing games, such as Dungeons & Dragons, which were also becoming popular with mainstream audiences at that time. I also mentioned above how strategy board games like Larry Harris's Axis and Allies (published by Nova Game Designs in 1981, then republished by Milton Bradley in 1984 as part of the "Gamemaster Series" of similar historically themed board games) could serve as an introduction to the larger, more established, and much more complex hobby of war gaming. Although we may be tempted to think that the fluidity between genres, modes, and styles of play is a relatively new development, it is clear that by the 1980s there were already many different ways to enter the realm of gaming—and I was obsessed with most of them.

I consider myself extremely fortunate to have grown up during the golden age of arcade games, as well as the rise of home video gaming with such home systems as the Atari 2600, Intellivision, and ColecoVision consoles, but my true gaming love is for the genre of role-playing games, which I also discovered during the 1980s, when the Dungeons & Dragons craze was sweeping the country. Originally conceived by E. Gary Gygax and Dave Arneson as a supplement to a set of rules for fantasy miniatures war gaming (aka "Chainmail"), Dungeons & Dragons, or D&D, grew into a successful series of Basic, Expert, and Advanced versions. There were several groups of kids in my elementary school who were playing D&D, and one of our sixth-grade teachers was known to run the game as Dungeon Master during lunchtime recess or occasionally after school. Soon I had my own copy of the Basic ruleset, otherwise known as the "Red Box," which came with a set of rules, a playable scenario known as a dungeon module, and seven plastic polyhedral dice—a four-sided die, a six-sided die, an eight-sided die, two ten-sided dice, a twelve-sided die, and of course the almighty d20 or twenty-sided die, which was rolled to resolve most basic actions in the game, including combat.

The dice were the cheapest kind of plastic and the numbers needed to be colored in with a crayon, but it didn't matter. I was hooked in the worst way, and quickly graduated from the Basic and Expert boxes to the so-called splatbooks of the Advanced Dungeons & Dragons ruleset: the Player's Handbook, which contained all of the information you needed to create your own fantasy adventurer character; the Monster Manual, which was an encyclopedic bestiary of creatures drawn both from various world mythologies as well as the fertile imaginations of Gygax, Arneson, and the other original founding fathers of AD&D; and last but not least the Dungeon Master's Guide, a massive tome stuffed to bursting with tables, charts, and lore for the Dungeon Master, who was responsible not just for adjudicating the game but who served as chief intermediary between the other players and the fictional universe of the fantasy role-playing game. (There are other books, of course—the creepy Fiend Folio detailing monsters created by D&D enthusiasts in the United Kingdom; Unearthed Arcana, a rulebook that for the first time introduced new rules, character classes, spells, and magic items to the Advanced D&D game and introduced the concept of an evolving set of rules for a role-playing game which is now in its fifth edition; and the infamous Deities & Demigods, which presented the gods and goddesses of various world religions in the style of the Monster Manual and probably helped stoke the moral panic that arose in the 1980s that D&D was somehow encouraging Satanism, witchcraft, or some unhealthy and antisocial combination of the two.)

Part referee, part storyteller, the Dungeon Master was the creator of his or her own universe, and although I enjoyed partaking of the game as a player, it was as Dungeon Master that I fell in love with D&D and the world of role-playing games. Standing behind my Dungeon Master's screen, which was a folding cardboard barrier set between my players and myself and festooned with important charts and tables culled from the rules, I felt like nothing less than a god. I even liked to put little skull-and-cross-bone stickers on my screen to tally all of the characters I had managed to kill during our mutual adventures, though in truth D&D was as much about collaboration between the players and Dungeon Master as it was conflict. The game itself came with a myriad of dungeon modules that had already been written for a Dungeon Master to run, including not just maps and lists of monsters, traps, and treasures that corresponded to numbered and lettered sections of the dungeons and other exotic and dangerous adventuring locales but also boxed "flavor text" that the Dungeon Master was supposed to read, as well as images that could be shared with the players when they reached certain points in the dungeon.

All of these were well and good—and in truth some of these published adventures are considered to be classics of the genre, such as the epic progressions of dungeon modules known as Against The Giants, which took players on a three-adventure quest that led to another trilogy of dungeon modules and a grand climax against Lloth, the Demon Queen of Spiders; or the stand-alone tournament module turned players' graveyard Tomb of Horrors, where players were challenged to their ultimate limits by a progression of increasingly unforgiving death traps—but the real potential of being a Dungeon Master lay in the ability to create one's own adventures. Dungeons & Dragons supposedly existed in a generic fantasy realm that drew heavily from Tolkien for its inspiration, but a truly ambitious Dungeon Master could imagine his own world instead, replete with its own imaginary history, its own politics, and even its own gods and goddesses. This is where Dungeons & Dragons transcended mere gameplay and became something else entirely than a simple set of rules. It was an experiment in a new kind of storytelling, one which would in turn inspire a new generation of authors—such as George R. R. Martin, whose wildly popular Song of Ice and Fire novels, set in the imaginary world of Westeros, were originally conceived as a "home-brewed" setting for his own established and long-running D&D campaign; China Mieville, writer in the genre of Weird Fiction whose tropes and world-building are derived heavily from his background in Dungeons & Dragons as a wildly creative and visionary Dungeon Master; as well as Junot Diaz, celebrated author of *The Brief Wonderful Life of Oscar Wao* and professor of literature at the Massachusetts Institute of Technology, who celebrated the escapist and liberating potential of D&D in a 2014 interview with the *New York Times*:

> When he was an immigrant boy growing up in New Jersey, the writer Junot Díaz said he felt marginalized. But that feeling was dispelled somewhat in 1981 when he was in sixth grade. He and his buddies, adventuring pals with roots in distant realms—Egypt, Ireland, Cuba and the Dominican Republic—became "totally sucked in," he said, by a "completely radical concept: role-playing," in the form of Dungeons & Dragons.
>
> Playing D&D and spinning tales of heroic quests, "we welfare kids could travel," Mr. Díaz, 45, said in an email interview, "have adventures, succeed, be powerful, triumph, fail and be in ways that would have been impossible in the larger real world.
>
> "For nerds like us, D&D hit like an extra horizon," he added. The game functioned as "a sort of storytelling apprenticeship." (Gilsdorf 2014)

We will discuss the salutary effects of gaming at various points in this book, and at length in chapter 2 when we will explore strategies in introducing games and gaming collections to your library's stakeholders, but let it suffice to say for now that it is hard to dispute that this one particular genre of gaming presents a wealth of creative possibilities when transplanted into a library setting. Consider for a moment the various cross-disciplinary activities and programming that could arise from a successful role-playing gaming presence at the library—from the obvious literary and media connections to the facilitated storytelling opportunities for teens and other demographics and the connections to local hobbyists in your community as well as your MakerSpace with the creation and construction of miniatures, dioramas, and other D&D peripherals that serve as tangible supplements to the pen and paper game. Dungeons & Dragons is capable of spawning its own creative ecosystem within the walls and stacks of your library, and all of this coming from just one game in one genre. Think about how other games may be able to transform your library community as well.

When I came to the Westport Library as director of knowledge curation and innovation, one of my first charges was to expand our range of experiential learning activities into the realm of gaming. Almost immediately after taking the job I did two things to that end. First, I signed myself up to attend Trade Day at GenCon, the largest gaming convention in the world held every year in Indianapolis during the first half of August. The convention also sponsors a mini-conference for librarians, game store owners, and other people who work on the "trade" side of the gaming industry a day before the actual gaming convention begins—if you mean to start your own gaming program at your library, this is a great opportunity to meet with those librarians who are already successfully doing so and pick their brains in a smaller, more intimate venue than most other library conferences.

And second, I bought the library a used copy of Fireball Island off of eBay. As soon as it arrived, we unboxed it with great fanfare. A couple of my staff members remembered playing this game as kids and looked on with a sense of childlike wonder as they were hit by this tangible blast from the past, but the vast majority of our staff and volunteers in our MakerSpace had simply never seen such a game before and were immediately fascinated by it. We had our inaugural run of Fireball Island right there in the middle of the library's common area, right behind the MakerSpace, where anyone could wander by, see what we were up to, and ask whatever questions they may have had about what we were up to, what Fireball Island was, and of course most importantly why we were playing it here in the library. No sooner did we finish our first game then we realized we had stumbled upon something of great inspiration and potential for our library, one that would kick off a year of creative innovation surrounding bringing games and gaming materials into our library community.

By the end of the year, we had successfully established a small circulating collection of board games in collaboration with our county gaming Meetup, reached out to our local friendly neighborhood gaming store and a regional artist and sculptor to initiate a wildly successful miniature painting series, sponsored at least two board game takeover events in our library in conjunction with national and international gaming awareness movements, organized and played our first library-sponsored Dungeons & Dragons campaign, successfully run several gaming "tavern nights" for members of our extended gaming and Maker community, and, perhaps most importantly, introduced many members of the library staff to the previously unfamiliar world of gaming—in particular, the genre of board gaming, using Fireball Island as our point of entry for new staff. We found that not only did our staff take to playing Fireball Island, but it proved to be a fun way to break the ice with our fellow employees by transporting ourselves four at a time into a friendly but competitive social environment. Staff members who showed interest in continuing their education in board gaming could then move on to more advanced fare, especially Pandemic, a popular cooperative game that proved to be of particular interest for our library and one that we will explore at greater length for its usefulness in team-building on the job and its creative potential for MakerSpaces with the introduction of its breakaway best-selling Legacy variant, which turns the very notion of board games on its head and elevates them, like role-playing games, into their own narrative plane.

But bringing Fireball Island to the library was also just about the fun. This is a point that I feel bears repeating as much as I possibly can, so please bear with me if you hear me say this a hundred more times before this book has reached its conclusion: libraries should be fun. People who feel otherwise aren't just wrong; they misunderstand the primary function of a library to its community as a safe space for experimentation and play with new ideas. It doesn't matter where these new ideas come from. A long time ago libraries were all about printed books and the library did its best to leverage the risk of owning all of these items (or by borrowing them via such mechanisms at Interlibrary Loan, that wonderful and magical reciprocal ability of libraries to rely on one another to help fill the gaps on their respective collections) on its patrons' behalf; now we buy DVDs, ebooks, laptops, tablets, and wearable technology—even telescopes. Why should games be any different? But at the same time, games are different because unlike these other library materials games make no bones about being first and foremost all about having fun. This is a radical notion, but one that by the end of this book I hope you will agree with me is wholly consistent with the mission of libraries as a playground for new ideas. Play has always been an unspoken partner of libraries, so while naysayers may try to convince you that games and gaming have no place in the library, it is my fervent hope that over the next hundred or so pages, you will find yourself not just impassioned to rebut these wrong-headed critiques but comprehensively armed and empowered to do so.

As librarians we ignore games and gaming at our own peril. Already the academy has begun to embrace the study of games just as they begrudgingly accepted television, media, and even comic books each in turn as legitimate forms of literature. Gaming literacy is already the default literacy for an entire generation of white American males, and as the appeal of gaming increasingly crosses into other demographics, we must prepare ourselves for a world where games are just one of several equally valid forms of discourse. Because gaming is still not without its attached stigmas and social prejudices, however, libraries often feel a strong counterpressure against recognizing gaming literacy, especially as some stakeholders believe that games are ultimately frivolous and a waste of time, with no redeeming social value at best and having a quantifiable negative effect on gamers at worst. While I hope we will be able to happily dismiss the latter fear as so much nonsense, it will be more of a challenge to demonstrate the social and intellectual utility of games, but one that I believe is ultimately surmountable over the next several chapters. Whether or not you will be able to carry the day at your own institution in opening your patrons, staff, and other stakeholders to the usefulness of games and gaming remains to be seen, but if nothing else please try to draw comfort from the understanding that this is an ideal that is still in its infancy but is ultimately destined to win out in the long run.

The moral? Always bet on the side of fun! Your staff, stakeholders, patrons, and community will thank you.

◎ The Road Ahead

This book will begin with an overview of gaming in libraries in chapter 1, both historical and contemporary, followed by how to make your case for introducing library gaming programming to your community in chapter 2. Once you've gotten that green light to proceed, in chapter 3 we'll talk about how to assemble your collection of games, followed by the mechanics of circulating and caring for a library games collection in chapter 4, and then a how-to for crafting new library gaming programming, evaluating and assessing existing gaming events and activities, and using data and feedback to grow your collections, programs, and services in chapter 5.

Chapters 6 through 10 will cover specific kinds of games and gaming activities, from board games to video games to mobile augmented reality games such as Pokémon GO to role-playing games and finally library pub quiz or trivia games. In chapter 11 we will look more closely at how your library gaming program can collaborate with your MakerSpace or experiential learning staff in supporting any of the games mentioned in the previous chapters.

Reference

Gilsdorf, Ethan. 2014. "A Game as Literary Tutorial: Dungeons & Dragons Has Influenced a Generation of Writers." *The New York Times*, July 13. www.nytimes.com/2014/07/14/books/dungeons-dragons-has-influenced-a-generation-of-writers.html.

Acknowledgments

People whom I'd like to thank:

- My parents, who hid that Atari 2600 console from me so well on that Christmas morning all those years ago that I really didn't think I was going to get it.
- My wife, Maria, who is so not a gamer but has never objected to my passing on the gamer gene to both of our children.
- My daughter, Andriana, for being as fiercely competitive a board gamer as she is an athlete.
- My son, Mario, for all the games we will play together in the future.
- My sixth-grade teacher, Mr. Tracy, who initiated a generation of kids into the mysteries of Dungeons & Dragons (who in turn lured me in!).
- My best friend, Mark, with whom I've been playing D&D since 1990.
- Alex Giannini, my partner in crime. Thank you for the best year of my library career.
- Jaina Shaw and Melanie Kelly, who wrote the best trivia questions of all time.
- My editor, Ellyssa Kroski, who has the patience of a saint. This was a crazy time for me, but you always knew exactly what to say to keep me writing!
- The makers of Fireball Island: Bruce Lund and Chuck Kennedy.

CHAPTER 1

A Short History and Survey of Gaming in Libraries

IN THIS CHAPTER

▷ Gaming Is Nothing New

▷ Checkmate to Vice? Chess in the Library

▷ Chess Club Resources

▷ Synergy with Collection Development and Other Programming

▷ Don't Forget the Puzzles!

▷ Too Much of a Good Thing? Crossword and Contest Puzzles

▷ From Moral Improvement to Recreation?

▷ Libraries and the Gaming Renaissance

▷ Circulating Board Games

▷ A Library Retro Video Game Paradise

▷ Dungeons & Dragons: Bringing Your d20 to the Library

▷ Escape the Library

My daughter, Andriana, and I play chess outdoors in Niantic, Connecticut.

Gaming Is Nothing New

WHILE IT IS TEMPTING TO THINK of gaming in libraries as a relatively recent phenomenon, almost the opposite is true: for almost as long as we've had libraries, games and gamers have had some kind of presence there. In fact, the oldest continuously running chess club in the United States, located at the Mechanics' Institute Library in San Francisco, was founded in 1854! As librarian, author, and gaming expert Scott Nicholson observes, using gaming to lure people away from the debauchery of the public house was wholly consistent with the nineteenth-century public library's mission to elevate the moral health of the community (Nicholson 2013). Although we no longer necessarily associate gaming with virtue—in many cases it's actually quite the opposite, with gaming often being unfairly associated with addictive and antisocial behaviors—the allure of gaming has persisted as a tool for bringing patrons into the library. Ironically enough, however, the more we learn about the effect of playing games on the human brain, the more salutary effects we discover, with the result that the inclusion of gaming in libraries as a way toward personal betterment has come full circle.

In this chapter we will take a look at the origin and growth of gaming in libraries, from chess clubs to toy libraries and LAN parties to Laser Tag in the Stacks. We will also undertake a survey of libraries that are currently at the cutting edge of incorporating games and gaming into their collections and programming. Since this book is intended to be a practical guide and not a scholarly treatise, our historical perspective will be more of a whirlwind tour than an in-depth investigation—the same will be true for our global survey of current library gaming. For those of you who are interested in undertaking a deeper dive into this subject, please consult the bibliography at the end of this book.

Checkmate to Vice? Chess in the Library

With only a few notable exceptions—such as an incident in 1992 when a public library in New Rochelle, New York, had a patron arrested for playing chess in the reference area—

chess and libraries have enjoyed an almost symbiotic relationship over the years, with the majority of public libraries in the United States hosting some kind of organized chess club, chess classes, or simply unorganized open play. As such, chess represents the perfect "gateway game" for libraries seeking to expand their gaming offerings, as it shows that a library can invest in and accommodate their community's interests beyond supposedly traditional library offerings without the sky falling or the world coming to an end. In the next chapter, we will explore how to make your case for gaming in the library, but it should not come as a surprise that one of our chief points will be to leverage either your own local successes or those of your neighbors or your peer group. Notwithstanding the chess maven who got arrested in New Rochelle, chess is an extremely nonproblematic addition to the library on several fronts:

- The material needs for chess are almost negligible, as chess sets are ubiquitous and cheap (they can even be printed on your library's 3-D printer if you have one in your MakerSpace!). Moreover, many chess players will bring their own chess set to the library in order to play.
- The space needed for chess is limited—just enough room for two seated players and a board. It is therefore easy to accommodate an entire chess class or even a tournament with minimal muss and/or fuss on the library's part: simply add more tables and chairs as needed.
- Chess is regarded as a relatively quiet pastime, so that the potential disruption on the rest of the library's patrons is quite small. Note that in the case of actual instruction or particularly heated competition, chess may actually become loud enough to disturb the relative peace, but as far as games go, it's hard to find a less noisy exemplar.
- Chess is also thought of as a cerebral game, with a complicated set of rules to master and literally centuries of strategy to study when learning how to advance one's play from that of a beginner to a more serious and competitive level. As the website Chess Express Ratings says: "The benefits of chess may not be obvious to the library. At the very least, chess encourages concentration, focus, logic and decision-making; teaches cause and effect; rewards planning ahead and strategy, patience and playing by a set of rules, and respect for others. Losing games is part of playing chess, and learning from one's losses and handling them graciously are more benefits of chess that carry through to life in general" (Chess Express Ratings 2018).

This sense of chess being inherently "good for you" is in a sense a holdover from nineteenth-century attitudes about games being used as a vehicle for self-improvement, but it still resonates among library patrons who might otherwise dismiss the introduction of other forms of recreation into the library space. The trick for the would-be gaming librarian is to extend this aura of "embitterment [*sic*]" to other kinds of games.

⑥ Chess Club Resources

What if your library doesn't already have a chess club? You might want to see first if anyone in the community is already hosting chess-related events and reach out to them to ask if they would consider the library as a potential cohost. The United States Chess Federation keeps online lists of chess clubs and other U.S. Chess affiliates, as well as calendars for upcoming tournaments and national events of importance to U.S. Chess, including competitive events featuring prize money. As public space is often at a premium in many communities, the library can bring a lot to the table in this regard as an incentive for a group to bring their meetings to the library. If there are no formal chess groups in your community, you may want to consider testing the waters before committing the library to a permanent recurring program. International Games Week (née International Games Day @ Your Library—more about this in chapter 7) and other onetime events are excellent opportunities for offering chess instruction or free play to help gauge any potential interest; it is also an outreach opportunity for you and the local chess community, who might be able to connect you with players, instructors, and other interested parties who might be looking for a more organized presence.

⊚ Synergy with Collection Development and Other Programming

Not surprisingly, with a history as rich as that of chess, many books have been written on the subject—not only instructional and strategy guides on how to play chess, mind you, but also literature and other media about chess itself. There is even a musical written about the game—titled simply *Chess*—by Benny Andersson and Björn Ulvaeus of the pop group ABBA, with lyrics by Tim Rice, which is a tale of espionage, romance, and of course chess set during the height of the Cold War. The opportunities for collaborating with your subject librarians on collection development, media displays, and online guides are myriad, as is the potential for working with your MakerSpace or other experiential learning staff on chess-related programming.

We have already mentioned the possibility of printing out chess pieces on a 3-D printer. There are almost limitless variants to chess pieces, including themed chess sets with specialty pieces depicting a wide range of characters including historical figures, video game characters, or even the heroes and villains from *Star Wars*. The patterns for these pieces can either be found online (on websites such as Thingverse or Shapeways) or designed by library staff or volunteers and either printed, carved, sculpted, or even assembled with LEGO bricks. The opportunities for combining chess with hands-on making activities are truly boundless. We will revisit how your library's MakerSpace can supplement and bolster your gaming offerings in chapter 14, including how to create giant-sized versions of board games such as chess to reintroduce familiar gaming concepts in a way that is fresh and exciting for all audiences.

⊚ Don't Forget the Puzzles!

Another variety of gaming that has been a historic staple in libraries is the puzzle. How many public libraries right now have a table dedicated to a jigsaw puzzle in progress, woe be to anyone who dares disturb the solution in progress or, God forbid, loses a piece of the puzzle! Again, many libraries that don't otherwise have games or gaming programming nevertheless may have a small selection of jigsaw puzzles available for patrons to assemble, which goes to show how accepted the puzzle is in the culture of the public library. While we do not have a formative historical event commemorating the arrival of the first puzzle in a U.S. library as we do with the Mechanics' Library chess club, jigsaw puzzles hit their stride in the early 1900s, when the ability to mass-produce puzzles launched a national puzzle craze. By the 1930s, companies such as Parker Brothers were contributing to a market that sold ten million jigsaw puzzles a week.

Why were puzzles such a cultural phenomenon? Some credit the Great Depression for the sudden interest in puzzles, which offered a cheap alternative to other forms of entertainment such as the cinema, restaurants, and night clubs. Puzzles also offered a kind of mental challenge and a sense of accomplishment upon completion, again making it a more "virtuous" pastime than other more morally unsavory options. Whatever the underlying reasons, puzzles were in such demand that local craftsmen would create their own and libraries added circulating jigsaw puzzles to their collections, sometimes charging a nominal rental fee to loan them depending on size (Williams 2017). This is an interesting early example of libraries meeting the expectations and needs of their community to provide nontraditional materials. Then just as now there were people who wagged their tongues at the idea of libraries spending money to make these kinds of realia available to the public, the objection being that funds being used to purchase puzzles could have been redeployed to buy books instead. Instead of being discouraged that this argument has always taken place in the public library, perhaps we should draw comfort from the fact that even then librarians were able to prevail in meeting their patrons' needs, not just for information but for other materials that they deemed important to be able to offer to the community. There may always be naysayers, but as said curmudgeons did not prevail back then over the issue of circulating jigsaw puzzles, let us be more confident that we will be able to make our own cases for supporting other kinds of gaming materials in the library as well.

Too Much of a Good Thing? Crossword and Contest Puzzles

Another kind of puzzle is the contest puzzle, which could take many different forms, including its perhaps most popular format: the crossword puzzle. Like the jigsaw puzzle, contest puzzles became a cultural phenomenon during the Great Depression, but whereas the jigsaw puzzle was a time-consuming and stimulating way to engage idle hands, the prize monies associated with contest puzzles—which even by 1930s standards were significant—meant that people down on their luck could try supplementing their meager incomes by completing such challenges. According to Scott Nicholson, the pressures that these patrons placed on their local public library's resources were significant enough that many libraries were forced to place limits on the amount of time that certain reference items, such as dictionaries, could be used!

Today the daily crossword is still a staple for many and a library gaming staple as well, with many libraries hosting crossword contests that draw competitors from far and wide to try their luck and test their puzzle acumen. *New York Times* crossword puzzle editor and founder of the American Crossword Puzzle Tournament Will Shortz has made something of a cottage industry of supplying libraries with unpublished *NYT* crossword puzzles for these events and has even been known to host a library event every now and then at both public and academic libraries, including the Westport Library in Westport, Connecticut, and the Lilly Library at Indiana University at Bloomington.

From Moral Improvement to Recreation?

It wasn't until the postwar period that gaming in libraries began to shift toward an emphasis on recreation instead of betterment, but even then the moral dimension of games was a major factor in their inclusion. Scott Nicholson points to two library science articles, written in 1942 and 1966, that made the case for including games of skill for social and mental recreation and identified gaming as a way to lure in groups of patrons who were not typical library users. At some point between then and now, the primary purpose of including gaming in libraries shifted from that of moral improvement to that of outreach. Since patrons who come to the library in order to play games were more likely to use the library's resources and materials in other respects as well—or so the reasoning went—then gaming was acceptable as a means of getting those patrons in the door. It would be several decades yet before librarians would make a serious argument for a broader definition of literacy that would embrace gaming, but in the meantime it was enough that gaming in the library was taking place in an environment that was "literacy-positive."

Even though the concept of the public library as a center for moral improvement was starting to wane, the space race heralded by the Soviet launch of Sputnik into low Earth orbit placed a new emphasis on American technological ingenuity. Although libraries these days make a big to-do about their embrace of STEM (or nowadays STEAM, throwing the arts back into the mix as well), public libraries in the 1960s, 1970s, and even the 1980s were already supplementing the science and educational curricula of their community's school systems. This change in focus helped some libraries embrace gaming—especially video gaming, which was just coming of age in the late 1970s and the early 1980s with the first generation of consumer console games and personal computers becoming commercially available—but even with this powerful argument in favor of bringing in games under the aegis of science and technology education, many libraries continued to view board games, role-playing games, and video games as distractions at best and wholly incompatible with the public library's mission and vision at worst.

Libraries and the Gaming Renaissance

But all is not an uphill battle for the would-be gaming librarian. The twenty-first century has brought some significant changes in how the public uses libraries and how libraries are positioning themselves within their communities, with many of these changes tilting in favor of gaming. Moreover, there are many examples of libraries that have championed games and made gaming an integral part of their collections, programming, and services. While an exhaustive list of these libraries is beyond the scope of this book, let us conclude this chapter with a brief survey of some of the more successful endeavors in libraryland.

Circulating Board Games

In Bensalem, Pennsylvania, the Bucks County Library System has more than 150 modern board games as part of its circulating board game collection, with new games being added to this already burgeoning collection every year. The result of a pilot program that demonstrated community interest and viability of the concept, the circulating board game collection now encompasses all six branches with a $3,000 annual budget for new acquisitions and other incidental costs (such as corner bands to hold game boxes tightly together, small bags for components, and labels for inventory lists). The collection started with just six core titles: Forbidden Island, Ticket to Ride, Carcassonne, Splendor, Catan, and Pandemic. All of them are considered to be "gateway" games—in other words, games that help introduce people to the basic concepts, gameplay, and strategy that make modern board gaming different than, say, playing Candy Land or Monopoly with your family.

Although the collection has grown by a couple of orders of magnitude, it is interesting to note that these gateway games are usually among the highest-circulating game titles for the collection.

The Bucks County Library System also supports their gaming collection with five different board game events, each tailored to a different segment of the library and local gaming communities. For example, there is a Board Game Night for Adults, one for Family Game Nights, a "Golden Gamers" group for ages sixty-five and older, a Game Designer Guild for would-be game designers to playtest and beta-test their games, and a recently added Winter Board Games Night, where the library takes its gaming collection to local bars and cafés for the evening. In short, gaming has been an overwhelming success at Bensalem and the other branches of the Bucks County Library System, as not only have they successfully included board games as part of their library collections but they have internalized gaming itself as an important aspect of the library system's identity. This institutional buy-in is a critical factor in their success—in the next chapter, we will discuss how to secure such buy-in from your own library administration, community, and stakeholders.

A Library Retro Video Game Paradise

The Mentor Public Library, located in Mentor, Ohio, puts a distinctive spin on their video game collections and programming, highlighting "retro" games such as Mario Bros., Pac-Man, and Galaga alongside events for current video game systems as well. With retro game events for both teens and adults, MPL encourages gamers of all ages to come to the library and square off playing against one another. The library also offers a Time Travelers Club, which introduces teens to classic games and crafts from different eras, including old-school video games and historical board games.

As Justin Hoenke, executive director of the Benson Memorial Library in Titusville, Pennsylvania, and one of the founding members of the library gaming advocacy group 8bitlibrary observes: "Due to their lack of retail availability, libraries can offer these [retro gaming] systems as part of the library collection and make them available for borrowing. Having the consoles also gives the library a chance to provide a more diverse array of video games. Since most public libraries were not collecting video games in the '80s and '90s, there is a lack of older titles in their collections. The NES and Super NES Classic offer a quick and easy way for them to fix that, so they're not just lending out the newest video games to their patrons" (Hoenke 2017).

Dungeons & Dragons: Bringing Your d20 to the Library

Every week at the Aberdeen Branch of the Harford County Public Library as many as fifteen to twenty teens gather to play Dungeons & Dragons with the teen librarian. The popular fantasy role-playing game now in its fifth edition, D&D "hits numerous tick boxes libraries strive for in their programming. [It is] an outlet for creativity, encourages social interaction between people of diverse backgrounds, and fosters reading comprehension and critical thinking skills" (Hutton 2017). What started as a modest campaign for a few recurring players has become one of the hot-ticket events for the library, with the game becoming so popular that they now offer two separate sessions—one run by the librarian, the other now run by a teen volunteer—and are contemplating adding a third.

The library also has the core D&D rulebooks as part of its circulating collections, so that teens interested in playing need not plunk down a good deal of money in order to learn how to play the game.

Several hundred miles to the west, another library D&D group tries to address the gender imbalance that often happens in the gaming genre, which can skew notably toward seeming to be a male-dominated boys' club. At the downtown main branch of the Public Library of Cincinnati and Hamilton County, a group called the Lady Knights runs a women-focused Dungeons & Dragons group for "ladies, genderqueer, agender and non-binary folks" ages fourteen and up. Another successful and popular program, the Lady Knights have recently had to switch to a bimonthly meeting schedule in order to meet demand to play in this gaming group, which offers a safe and supportive space for people who often feel marginalized in the D&D and RPG communities (Begley 2017).

Escape the Library

Finally let's take a look at one of the hottest trends in library gaming circles right now: escape rooms. Part puzzle, part live-action role-playing, escape rooms are physical adventure games where the players must solve a series of riddles or puzzles in order to escape a room or series of rooms. An outgrowth of a particular genre of video games, escape rooms come in a variety of different themes and styles—from zombie outbreaks to haunted houses, from prison breaks to science laboratories with experiments gone horribly awry, with some escape rooms even based on TV shows such as *Game of Thrones*—and have very quickly become a popular form of entertainment around the world. While many of these escape rooms are privately owned and operated and often cost a fee in order to play, libraries have started to create their own escape room games for their patrons to enjoy.

For example, at the Durham Public Library in Durham, Connecticut, patrons raced to find clues and solve the puzzles necessary to find the antidote to the zombie apocalypse in a recent series of escape room events. Part of the library's Halloween programming, their Escape Room Zombie Outbreak provided some immersive thrills and chills, while at the same time engaging library patrons with the mental challenge of solving the puzzles necessary to open the series of locks that would free the zombie antidote and allow the players to win the game.

It seems only fitting that we end this chapter with a return to the salutary nature of games, as this will be an important theme in chapter 2 as we discuss building the case for gaming at your own library. For now let us finish by reiterating that since the very beginning of public libraries in North America, gaming has had some kind of presence in the library space. Although the nature of that presence has changed over time, as has the justification for its inclusion in a library setting as well as whatever expenditures it would require to maintain, the constant presence of gaming should remind us that bringing games and game programming to your library isn't a new idea at all, but the homecoming of a very old one, indeed!

Key Points

- Gaming in libraries may seem like a new thing, but it has roots stretching back to the eighteenth century.

- Historically public libraries have both embraced and rejected gaming based on its positive or negative connotations—i.e., can gaming promote social or behavioral good—whereas modern analysis includes the importance of fostering creativity, structured play, and fun.
- Chess, puzzles, and crosswords are forms of gaming that many libraries already permit and can be used as leverage to include other forms of gaming.
- Gaming can be used to attract "missing" or underrepresented demographics from the library's community, leading to increased usage of other library materials and services.
- Libraries have a unique opportunity to position themselves as gaming-friendly social institutions during a large-scale renaissance of gaming and mainstreaming of gamer culture.

References

Begley, Emily. 2017. "A Women-Centric Dungeons & Dragons Group Fosters Friendships and Fun at the Downtown Library." *CityBeat*, February 1. www.citybeat.com/arts-culture/culture/article/20850781/a-womencentric-dungeons-dragons-group-fosters-friendships-and-fun-at-the-downtown-library.

Chess Express Ratings. 2018. "Start a Scholastic Chess Club in a Library." *CXR* (website). www.cxrchess.com/StartALibraryScholasticClub.php (accessed January 2, 2018).

Durham Public Library. 2018. "Escape Room: Zombie Outbreak." *Durham Public Library* (website). www.durhamlibrary.org/library-escape-room (accessed January 2, 2018).

Hoenke, Justin. 2017. "Retro Gaming Gives Libraries a Boost." *Information Today, Inc.*, December 12. newsbreaks.infotoday.com/NewsBreaks/Retro-Gaming-Gives-Libraries-a-Boost-122162.asp.

Hutton, Jake. 2017. "Librarians Report: Dungeons and Dragons in the Library." *Games In Libraries* (blog), September 18. games.ala.org/librarians-report-dungeons-and-dragons-in-the-library.

Nicholson, Scott. 2013. "Playing in the Past: A History of Games, Toys and Puzzles in North American Libraries." *Library Quarterly* 83, no. 4 (October): 341–361.

U.S. Chess Federation. 2018. *U.S. Chess Federation* (website). new.uschess.org/home/ (accessed December 31, 2017).

Williams, Anne. 2017. "History of Puzzles." *Puzzle Warehouse* (website). www.puzzlewarehouse.com/history-of-puzzles (accessed January 2, 2018).

Making Your Case for Library Gaming Programming with Stakeholders

IN THIS CHAPTER

▷ The Times, They Are A-Changin'

▷ Games Are Good for You

▷ Games as a Social Good

▷ Teens and Games

▷ The Value of Gaming to the Library

▷ Addressing Naysayers

▷ Don't Forget to Ask Your Community What They Want!

▷ Getting Permission to Have Fun

The Times, They Are A-Changin'

ALTHOUGH AS LIBRARIANS WE ARE ACCUSTOMED to think of our profession as being constantly on the defensive against declining budgets and fragmented patron interest, the fact of the matter is that there has never been a better time to try and introduce games and gaming to your library. Not only have there been tectonic shifts in how public libraries are reimagining themselves to meet the needs of their communities in the twenty-first century, but gaming itself is in the middle of a transformation whereby board games, video games, and role-playing games, once considered the exclusive domain of "freaks and geeks," have increasingly become part of mainstream North American entertainment culture. If the nerds have truly inherited the earth, then surely making the case for library gaming programming must be a no-brainer at this point.

Right? Well, not quite. For all of their reputation as being on the cutting edge of innovation in the library world, public libraries can sometimes be weirdly conservative on certain points. Alas, one of these cultural blind spots revolves around gaming and in particular the issue of having fun in the library. In many institutions, there is still an unconscious or even conscious bias against committing taxpayer money to games and gaming activities. While I am not trying to write a manifesto about what public libraries should or shouldn't be, the question of whether gaming belongs in the library lies on one of the aforementioned fault lines of the massive shifts currently under way in public library circles. Insofar as you as the would-be gaming librarian will be wading into this conflict—which is about expectations as much as it is about dollars and cents—it is incumbent upon you to understand how to sell your ideas to both the cultural and financial skeptics among your staff, administrators, and community. Therefore the purpose of this chapter is to make you the best of all possible advocates for games and gaming at your library.

As if bringing gaming into the pantheon of library collections, services, and programming weren't enough, you will also need to be able to defend the still somewhat radical notion that libraries should be safe places for play as well. In the preface, I have already touched on the basic premise that libraries can and should be fun—in this chapter I will also build upon this notion so that you are better able to articulate it to your stakeholders and use it as a rallying cry for cultural change at your local public library. Speaking purely from personal experience, nothing can truly prepare you for the first time you are challenged for daring to have fun at your place of employment while on the clock, as it seems to run antithetical to everything we understand about the nature of work and our concomitant expectations that govern the workplace, but I will do my best to prepare you not only for that challenge but the larger conversation about the interplay (pun intended) between work and fun of which the issue of gaming in the library strikes at the very heart.

Games Are Good for You

In the journal *PLOS One*, a team of neuroscientists recently concluded an experiment where a group of older adult subjects were asked to play Super Mario 64—a classic platform video game for the Nintendo 64 console and the first game in the long-lived Mario franchise to utilize 3-D graphics—over a six-month training period. When these subjects' brains were measured via MRI scans, they found that there had been a significant increase in the grey matter within the hippocampus, leading to enhanced spatial memory and navigation in the test subjects (West et al. 2017).

The benefits don't just stop with video games, however: according to a study in the *New England Journal of Medicine*, playing board games was linked with a lesser likelihood of developing dementia and Alzheimer's disease later in life (Verghese et al. 2003). Board games are also associated with improving logical reasoning and deduction skills, and playing chess has been linked to higher math scores on standardized tests (Barrett and Fish 2011).

Similar studies have been conducted measuring the impact of games on other kinds of cognitive and motor functions, and as the body of research grows, it becomes increasingly difficult to ignore the fact that the evidence overwhelmingly suggests that games are in fact objectively good for you.

⊚ Games as a Social Good

Aside from producing measurable improvement on the brain and its functioning, games also come with a host of social benefits as well. Not only do games foster a sense of community (or, in the case of video games, virtual community), but certain games can promote teamwork and communication skills, improve self-esteem, and help ward off depression. Role-playing games such as Dungeons & Dragons can help players develop their skills at problem-solving, creative expression, and even dealing with interpersonal conflict. Moreover, a 2006 study by researchers in Spain showed that the act of storytelling itself engaged areas of the brain that were otherwise unused (Gonzalez et al. 2006). Long gone are the days when public librarians were obliged to defend the inclusion of popular fiction to their library stacks—as it turns out, the same beneficial effects we derive from reading a good story can be derived from telling a good story as well.

There are other ancillary benefits to gaming, of course. If we had more than just this chapter to enumerate these positive effects, we could easily fill this entire book and then some! Games not only encourage perseverance and teach us how to learn from our failures, but they even help make us more likely to act competently in the event of an actual real-world crisis. One recent study showed that when someone is being physically harmed, eleven out of twenty gamers would intervene to help, as opposed to seven out of twenty nongamers (Tassi 2012).

⊚ Teens and Games

Amanda Schiavulli, member services librarian in the Finger Lakes System in New York, translates these various benefits linked to games and gaming into educational terms, showing that library gaming activities can achieve many of the forty Developmental Assets for Adolescents developed by the Search Institute, including Achievement Motivation (#21), Learning Environment Engagement (#22), Planning and Decision-Making (#32), Interpersonal Competence (#33), Personal Power (#37), and Self-Esteem (#38) (Schiavulli 2013). Schiavulli also links gaming—in particular video games—to higher levels of literacy, as more than one-third of gamers regularly read game-related texts including game reviews, strategy websites, fan fiction, and forum discussions. As former ALA literacy officer Dale Lipschulz put it: "Gaming—board, social, and video—is a meaningful literacy activity. Kids (and adults) are invested in gaming. It's fun, it's what they do with their peers, and they like it. Therefore it has meaning in their lives. Gaming usually requires some reading and writing skills. It always involves problem solving and strategy skills. Even reluctant readers will read and problem solve in order to 'level up' and master the game and stay competitive with their peers. That said, along with mastering the game, they are improving their basic skills" (Levine 2008).

With the competition of cheap books via Amazon and instant-gratification research options via Google, teen library usage has been steadily declining. Gaming, however, has the ability to reverse this trend and draw teens and their parents into the library. We have already mentioned how there is evidence that gaming and other programming for teens and other underserved demographics can translate into increased usage of traditional library materials and services—in other words, getting people inside your library's doors is more than half of the battle. Indeed, we do know in the case of teen library patrons that they are more likely to ask for help from a familiar face, so this is a strong point in favor of having library staff as involved in your gaming programming as possible, not simply providing oversight and material support but to facilitate gameplay, teach newcomers how to play, and even play themselves (Techsoup For Libraries). Enlisting teens to assist with the planning and execution of library gaming programming and events not only draws kids into the library's social sphere, but it also promotes good work/life skills as well as helping teens learn the logistics of developing, supporting, and carrying out these kinds of events.

⊚ The Value of Gaming to the Library

Sometimes it's easier to make the case for gaming in libraries by flipping the script—in other words, instead of saying, "Why should the library include gaming?" reframe the question as "What benefits does gaming bring to the library?" On the website for the ALA Games and Gaming Round Table, they ask this very question and provide the following succinct but compelling answers:

- New users (who may not visit the library) attend and gain insight into how the library may be relevant to them.
- Regular users may see the library in a new light.
- All users may be prompted to use other non-gaming library services.
- Ideally, all users have a positive library experience.
- Gaming programs epitomize library as 3rd place, creating a community place between home and work/school to socialize and play.
- Some videogame events are also being used to encourage print literacy. In Carver's Bay (SC), youth who check out books and write book reviews earn extra gaming time.
- Some videogame events may be educational in nature. Some libraries are teaching game design with local experts or online through Youth Digital Arts Cyber School.

I would add to this list an eighth response: "Some game events may have an experiential learning component, with opportunities for additional hands-on activities with the library's MakerSpace or experiential learning staff." More about the relationship between library gaming programming and MakerSpaces appears in chapter 11.

⊚ Addressing Naysayers

Thus far we have restricted ourselves to listing the positive attributes of gaming and its applicability to the public library setting. However, as an advocate for gaming at your library, you should be prepared for people to challenge you on the basic premise that games have any place in the library. These challenges may come from surprising quarters—not just a curmudgeonly patron but one of your coworkers, a vocal supporter of the library from your community, even your own boss or one of your library board members. The most important thing to remember when answering such complaints is that you are first and foremost an ambassador for gamers and that by taking their objections personally, you run the risk of only confirming people's worst stereotypes about gamers and the gaming community at large: that they are disruptive and antisocial and lack basic empathy for other people. While these beliefs are easily demonstrated to be false, first impressions are nevertheless very difficult things to overcome, and by not engaging your stakeholders as equals, you are depriving yourself of a valuable opportunity to listen to your constituents.

Instead of coming up with my own imperfect list, I would defer once again to the ALA Games and Gaming Roundtable, which has the following responses to several common objections from community members regarding the inclusion of gaming in the library:

- Games are fluff or junk entertainment
  Some are! So are many books. There is a serious games initiative in the gaming industry, and many games have an edutainment flair.
- Games don't encourage original thought
  Although a gamer may follow a path laid out by a designer, they are often several ways to get to the endgame. Playing a game requires creativity and imagination.
- Games don't offer learning opportunities
  Steven Berlin Johnson says that playing a game is like engaging the scientific method: a constant hypothesize/experiment/evaluate process. You learn something new every time.
- Games are competing with books
  It's not books OR games, it's books AND games.
- Games are a replacement for traditional print literacy
  Literacy is changing—there is a new literacy now. Today's youth must be fluent in visual literacy, media literacy, social literacy . . .
- All games are violent like Grand Theft Auto
  85% of games have content that is NOT rated M for mature. GTA represents a very small portion of available videogames. No one objects to chess, the game that has been playing in libraries the longest; CHESS is a war game that involves "killing" your opponent's army and monarchy.
- Games are addictive
  Many games are! Some offer immediate rewards and many require concentrated effort. Many encourage self-improvement. Games may be especially addictive for some personality types: moderating gameplay time, interspersing gaming with other activities, and playing with other people helps. Parents and adults need to set appropriate time limits for youngsters, and encourage a balanced media diet.
- Games are too passive
  Compared with TV, movies, or even books? Moreover, games like Dance, Dance Revolution or the games of Wii Fit can be quite physically demanding.

⊚ Don't Forget to Ask Your Community What They Want!

Okay, you've considered the pros and cons of implementing gaming collections and programs at your library. Time to come up with an action plan. Before you cast your d20 and see whether fortune indeed favors the brave, you should make sure that there is community interest in gaming at the library in the first place. If you work at a library that already has experimented with some kind of gaming activities and achieved encouraging results, then in your case it is simply a matter of capitalizing on existing successes and leveraging them into new areas of innovation and growth. If you work at a library that has traditionally never offered this kind of programming, however, it can be frustrating to try to break through what feels very much like a chicken-and-egg scenario: how can you demonstrate community interest in something if the community doesn't even realize that this is a potential option? This just means you should be thinking in terms of onetime events and pop-up activities rather than committing yourself to a larger and potentially more time-consuming and/or expensive course of action.

How to craft gaming programming itself is a topic that we will address in greater detail in chapter 5, but for now the key point is to start small. It's easier to ramp up to meet demand than it is to cut back once you've committed resources, staff, and your own credibility to a new library project. Consider planning a library gaming day or night or some other onetime event where you can feature some games and gaming activities and see what the reaction is. If you have the discretionary budget to purchase materials at this stage, concentrate on games and game systems that are popular. For board games, try one of the "gateway" games such as Ticket to Ride, Settlers of Catan (or Catan), Pandemic, Carcassonne, or Forbidden Island. For video games, consider something from the Nintendo family of consoles, such as the Wii, Wii U, or Nintendo Switch, and a multiplayer game such as Mario Kart or Super Smash Bros. If you are in contact with a local gaming group, they may bring their own collection to the event and help introduce patrons to unfamiliar games. Also, if you are able to contact a friendly local game store, they might even be able to provide you with free or discounted games for the evening or at least lend their expertise in exchange for some free advertising at the library.

If the event is successful, consider making it a regularly recurring event—maybe it's a quarterly seasonal event, or perhaps it is a monthly meeting. You may want to consider tying your event to existing national or international gaming "holidays"—such as International Games Week or International Tabletop Day—in order to increase your exposure and leverage existing publicity already associated with these larger events. At any rate, once you start to grow beyond the occasional games day/night, you'll want to start putting together an action plan for something more ambitious, including enhancing your gaming collections and brainstorming new library gaming events in programming. I will cover how to add games to your library's collections through buying, borrowing, and other less orthodox means of acquisition in chapter 3. As mentioned earlier, in chapter 5 I will cover not only how to come up with a plan for library gaming programming but how to evaluate and assess it once you have your programming up and running so that it may dynamically reflect your community's interests and needs as they evolve along with their own expectations and as the gaming milieu continues to develop in new and exciting directions.

Getting Permission to Have Fun

In this chapter, we have looked at various methods of selling your stakeholders on the idea of starting a library gaming program, from affirmations of its potential salutary effects—both biological and social—to strategies for dealing with critics and naysayers. We have also shown how to test the waters with your community when starting a new gaming program from scratch, and in subsequent chapters we will address how to pay for your gaming collections (or not pay, if you're terribly clever) and how to come up with both event-based and recurring library gaming programs at your library. We will now conclude the chapter with making the case for having fun while you are busy putting all of this together and making it happen.

The notion that library work should be "fun" is still something of a radical concept, but elsewhere in the working world, the idea is beginning to take root. According to a recent poll, 60 percent of 2015 college graduates said that they would prefer a workplace with a "positive social atmosphere" even if it meant making less money (Oden-Hall 2017). So how do we make the library a fun place to work? Within the context of games and gaming, the answer is obvious: in order to encourage a culture of gaming at the library, you want to foster a gaming-positive environment among both library staff and your patrons. This means getting involved. Just as our community comes to the library for readers' advisory based on the supposition that librarians read extensively, keep up with the publishing industry, and are passionate about connecting patrons with the perfect book, we should be prepared to support gaming in libraries with an equal amount of expertise and enthusiasm.

In the case of library gaming programming, it is important for library staff to feel comfortable with helping patrons navigate the games in the library's collection. Consider hosting a staff-only games party in order to introduce your colleagues to your most popular board and video games so that they feel empowered to answer basic questions about the materials, just as they would be knowledgeable on some level about ebook readers, electronic resources, or how to operate the copy machine or scanner. Gaming together with library staff can help foster team-building as well as a shared sense of ownership over any new library gaming programming you may offer. Remember that, especially in the case of front-line staff, they are the people most likely to receive pointed questions about why the library is now investing the community's hard-earned tax monies into loaning out board games or hosting video game tournaments. The more library staff you are able to recruit to your cause, the easier it is to sell this culture to your patrons and extended library community.

This means making time for staff to play games on the company clock. If selling this idea to your boss or administration gives you pause, take a deep breath. While this is unfamiliar territory for many workplaces, you should try to approach securing the buy-in you need by proceeding along familiar lines. For example, if you sell introducing new games as a form of staff training, not only does this make thematic sense but there's also ample precedent for supporting this kind of activity. You may also want to consider a regular rotation of public service staff to assist with recurring library gaming programming, such as a monthly gaming night, so that staff who might not otherwise be exposed to certain kinds of games and gaming activities get an opportunity to learn about them as well.

Be mindful that, although gamers are a fairly self-selecting lot, gaming actually appeals to a significant portion of nongamers as well. A fair and balanced games training program for library staff should enlist both those who identify as gamers and those who do not. Again, the broader the segment of staff that you can involve in your library's gaming programming and activities, the more representative this activity will appear to the general public, encouraging participation by a broader demographic from the library's community and perhaps even inspiring people to leap out of their own comfort zones and join in the fun. Building a culture of fun in the library workplace will not happen overnight, but it is an achievable goal if you keep these things in mind and work toward a vision of equal-opportunity enjoyment.

ⓖ Key Points

- Modern neuroscience seems to suggest that playing games can have beneficial effects on cognition, spatial memory and reasoning, neuromotor skills, and reflexes.
- Although often viewed as being solitary in nature, gaming culture is increasingly social and can promote teamwork and communication skills.
- Library gaming programs for teens can achieve many of the forty Developmental Assets for Adolescents.
- Public libraries should accentuate the positive when highlighting what gaming can do for libraries but should also be prepared to address naysayers' or skeptics' objections.
- The best way to encourage staff buy-in for gaming programming at the library is to get them involved and gaming themselves!

ⓖ References

American Library Association Games and Gaming Round Table. 2015. "Obstacles and Challenges." *American Library Association* (blog). www.ala.org/rt/gamert/obstacles-and-challenges (accessed January 2, 2018).

Barrett, David C., and Wade W. Fish. 2011. "Our Move: Using Chess to Improve Math Achievement for Students Who Receive Special Education Services." *International Journal of Special Education* 26, no. 3: 181–193.

Gonzalez, Julio, Alfonso Barros-Loscertales, Friedemann Pulvermuller, Vanessa Meseguer, Ana Sanjuan, Vicente Belloch, and Cesar Avila. 2006. "Reading Cinnamon Activates Olfactory Brain Regions." *NeuroImage* 32, no. 2 (August 15): 906–912.

Levine, Jenny. 2008. "Does Gaming Promote Reading?" *The Shifted Librarian* (blog), April 15. theshiftedlibrarian.com/archives/2008/04/15/does-gaming-promote-reading.html.

Oden-Hall, Kathy. "Benefits of Fun in the Workplace." 2017. *Forbes*, February 9. www.forbes.com/sites/paycom/2017/02/09/benefits-of-fun-in-the-workplace/#3cbbbe7378b1.

Schiavulli, Amanda. 2013. "Gaming @ Your Library: A Look at Collections, Programming and Best Practices" (presentation). www.flls.org/wp-content/uploads/2013/03/Gaming-Presentation-2.21.14.pdf (accessed January 2, 2018).

Tassi, Paul. 2012. "The Social Benefits of Video Games." *Forbes*, March 22. www.forbes.com/sites/insertcoin/2012/03/22/the-social-benefits-of-video-games/#5f653a41259.

Techsoup For Libraries. "Gaming in Libraries." *Techsoup For Libraries* (website). www.techsoupforlibraries.org/planning-for-success/innovation/gaming-in-libraries (accessed January 2, 2018).

Verghese, Joe, Richard B. Lipton, Mindy J. Katz, Charles B. Hall,, Carol A. Derby, Gail Kuslansky, Anne F. Ambrose, Martin Sliwinski, and Herman Buschke. 2003. "Leisure Activities and the Risk of Dementia in the Elderly." *New England Journal of Medicine* 348: 2508–2516.

West, G. L., B. R. Zendel, K. Konishi, J. Benady-Chorney, V. D. Bohbot, I. Peretz et al. 2017. "Playing Super Mario 64 Increases Hippocampal Grey Matter in Older Adults." *PLOS One* 12, no. 12: e0187779.

CHAPTER 3

How to Acquire Games and Gaming Materials for Your Library with Minimal Overhead Cost

IN THIS CHAPTER

▷ A Plan for Every Budget

▷ Good News! Library Vendors Are Getting the Message

▷ Support Your Local Businesses

▷ Your Friendly Local Game Store: Friend or Foe?

▷ The Salvation Army and Beyond: Finding Discounted Games

▷ Borrowing Games—Wait, What?

▷ Why Not Just Donate Instead?

▷ You Wouldn't Download a Game, or Would You?

A Plan for Every Budget

ONE OF THE MOST DIFFICULT PARTS of launching any new library program or service is finding the money to get things started. In the case of games and gaming activities, however, the good news is that there are many ways to implement an effective and exciting library gaming program on a shoestring budget—or even for free, if you're willing to hustle. The most important thing to remember about acquiring games for your library is that new isn't always necessary and that even missing pieces and components can always be cheaply replaced or even crafted by your own library's MakerSpace (if you have one). Older games can be just as much fun to play as the latest offerings, especially in the case of video games, where retro chic rules.

In this chapter, we will look at the various methods of acquiring games and gaming materials for your library: buying from contracted vendors, making deals with local businesses and/or your friendly local game store, finding discounted games, borrowing games and gaming accessories, and soliciting donations for items or making your own. Please note that any of these strategies may work for any library, given the circumstances. Even a well-funded library should not hesitate to look for bargain acquisitions, and sometimes even for the most cash-strapped institution, there is no substitute for a quality investment every now and then.

Good News! Library Vendors Are Getting the Message

Chances are that your library already works with one or more vendors to provide streamlined and discounted acquisitions of library materials, be they books, journals, ebooks, DVDs, CDs, or audiobooks. As it turns out, these same vendors are starting to venture into supporting purchases for nontraditional library items as well, including games. You may not be able to find everything that you're looking for yet, but you will be able to take advantage of your normal streamlined acquisitions workflow, including ease of purchase if you work at a library where credit card or check purchases require jumping through myriad hoops when trying to add materials to the collection.

Vendors may also help you with discovery, as many will provide cataloging records for said materials, if available. Using a library vendor for games purchases may streamline the purchasing and post-receipt processing, but take care—sometimes your acquisitions budgets linked to vendor accounts are tied to specific material formats, so you may have to meet with your financial staff to make sure you are able to account for nontraditional library purchases in your budget.

Support Your Local Businesses

Another option for purchasing is to identify a partner in your community capable of meeting your game material needs, such as a bookstore, toy store, game store, or hobby supply shop. You may be able to set yourself up with a business-to-business account, which could not only provide you with discounted pricing but may open up other benefits as well, such as early access to premium titles. Partnering with community businesses also raises the possibility of joint library programming, either in terms of outreach (i.e., you bring the library to the store or shop for an event) or a gaming event where your partner provides free or discounted materials or expertise in exchange for free publicity.

Some companies will allow you to host a "games night" at your library, where the company provides demonstration games, promotional materials, and sometimes even logistical support in exchange for a percentage of game sales for the night. The proceeds of any games sales could then be used to fund future acquisitions for your game program. For example, Gamewright, an award-winning gaming company based in Newton, Massachusetts, that produces games for kids, preteens, and up (including Forbidden Island, a 2011 Spiel des Jahrers Finalist and Games Magazine Top 100 Game), will work with libraries, schools, and other nonprofit organizations to host Gamewright GameNights; other game companies will often do something along similar lines.

Why? Because boards games are still new enough that any exposure is good exposure and any sales are good sales. Also, libraries and educational institutions are great potential repeat customers for games, purchasing multiple copies for popular titles and replacement copies for well-loved games. Libraries also help introduce their communities to the company's deeper catalog of offerings and build hype for future releases. Many of the same reasons that book publishers will cooperate closely with libraries (i.e., not just as major purchasers but as advocates, taste-makers, and trusted voices among their communities) are even more valid for game companies.

⊚ Your Friendly Local Game Store: Friend or Foe?

Do you have a FLGS? It stands for friendly local game store, a term which has been used for decades to denote a local gaming outpost. As opposed to a bookstore, toy store, or hobby shop, which may carry games and gaming accessories along with other products, a FLGS is either devoted entirely to games or carries games and collectibles such as comic books. Your friendly local game store is usually a hub for local gaming activity as well—if the FLGS has space, it often hosts various community gaming events and perhaps even local tournaments; even if it lacks the physical space for this, it will often serve as a clearinghouse for gamers looking for gaming groups or gaming groups looking for gamers. The owners of a FLGS are almost always gamers themselves and as such are usually invaluable sources of information about the gaming hobby, how to play popular games, and what is trending among their customers.

There are two ways to think of your FLGS if you have one: either as your competition or your ally. After all, like independent bookstores, friendly local game stores are usually operating on something of a razor margin, so anything that seems like an attempt to poach their territory or clientele could be interpreted in the least flattering light. It need not be this way, however. Approached with all due respect for their business model, a FLGS can be a powerful ally in your quest to build quality library gaming programming, just as your library can help them by introducing your community to modern games and gaming culture. For example, you may be able to ask your FLGS for volunteers to assist with a "game night" activity or to provide discounts on materials purchased to supplement gaming events, such as miniatures, which are essentially components for both war gaming and role-playing gaming. Having experts from the gaming community on hand can help lend legitimacy and a sense of confidence to your event, just as it raises awareness among your library patrons about your friendly local game store.

There is still something of a delicate dance to be performed, though, as although many friendly local game stores offer space for gaming, these spaces are usually populated by a stereotypical "gamer" demographic—that is, white males between the ages of ten and thirty. The overwhelming majority of these customers are playing collectible card games, such as Magic: The Gathering or Yu-Gi-Oh!, or miniatures-based war games such as Warhammer 40k, although with the recent upswing in popularity in the fifth edition of Dungeons & Dragons, you may find some D&D groups on hand as well. Although these spaces are often considered to be oases for this demographic, it can sometimes be awkward or difficult for people who do not belong to this particular group to feel welcomed there. While gamers are often unfairly tarnished as being rude and/or socially awkward, there can at times be something of an insular "locker room" atmosphere at play so that even if no intentional harm is meant by certain kinds of jokes or behaviors, it may result in an exclusionary environment nevertheless.

This is of course where the public library can excel, as we have extensive experience in creating spaces where all people are welcome. If you wish to partner with your FLGS on offering events, see if you can alternate hosting collectible card games or Warhammer 40k events, so that you can help open up these hobbies beyond their traditional circle of enthusiasts without appearing as if you are trying to steal them from your partner—this may in turn spawn a virtuous cycle where your FLGS may see a more diverse crowd coming to shop and play at their store. The library can be a powerful tool for outreach in this way and a platform through which we can articulate and reinforce our community's values through positive affirmation.

The Salvation Army and Beyond: Finding Discounted Games

Aside from partnering up with local businesses, you can still often find deals on old or used games by hitting the thrift stores and other second-hand shops. Many online gaming forums are buzzing with tales of picking up even relatively new board games, video games, or even video game consoles from local Goodwill or Salvation Army thrift stores. Yard sales, estate sales, and flea markets are also a great source for cheap board games as well. The issue of missing pieces can usually be addressed through either an online supplier or by simply printing out the needed components on a 3-D printer, and rulebooks are almost always available in PDF format at that wondrous clearinghouse of gaming known as BoardGameGeek.com.

Speaking of online resources, eBay and Amazon Marketplace are two additional places to find cheap used games, except in the case of those items that are truly rare and are now considered collectible, such as our original board game example, Fireball Island. The aforementioned BoardGameGeek.com also has an extensive board game marketplace. Another alternative is Gamers Alliance (gamersalliance.com), a members-only gaming organization since 1986 whose master catalog of out-of-print games alone is worth the $25 annual membership fee.

But even large box stores occasionally put board games on clearance, with extensive markdowns available if you catch them at the right time. For example, Barnes & Noble will seasonally mark down select games and toys shortly before they bring out a new line of merchandise. Other stores such as Target and Walmart will occasionally run buy one, get one free or two-for-one sales on board games as well, so it pays to keep your eyes peeled and make your purchases when the time is right to maximize your gaming acquisitions bang for your buck.

Borrowing Games—Wait, What?

No, we're not talking about borrowing games from other organizations so that you can lend them to others, although such game loan subscription services do in fact exist—with companies such as Gamefly for video games and Tiki Tiki Board Games and Board Game Exchange for board games filling these particular market niches. Instead I'm suggesting that, instead of purchasing the initial offerings for your library game collection, you ask community members either to lend or donate their own board games to the cause instead.

Obviously loaning something like a board game to a circulating service can be a dangerous prospect, with the odds of some components getting lost along the way or just worn down through wear and tear being fairly high, but considering what kind of model you are adopting for your game loans (i.e., circulating vs. in-house collections, which we'll discuss in chapter 4), soliciting loaner games, or gaming consoles in the case of video games, might just be a way to jump-start your collection until you are able to secure funding for the library's own items. It is important if you are borrowing materials from patrons or library staff members that the terms of the loan are clear and that you have spelled out which party is responsible in the case of damage or loss. I would only recommend this approach in the case of a carefully controlled circulation environment— either a closed circulation model for a closed game group or a noncirculating, demonstration-only gaming activity.

In the case of rare and/or expensive games, however, this might be the only opportunity to highlight such a game in a library activity. For example, take our collectible board game Fireball Island: the library may not be able to afford a copy of the game, but perhaps there is a local game collector who is willing to make it available for patrons to play for a special event; you could also imagine an identical scenario for a vintage arcade video game or a top-of-the-line virtual reality headset. If a member of the community is willing to share such an experience with other library patrons in a controlled and supervised environment, then this represents a win-win situation for everyone involved and might inspire library stakeholders that they should in fact invest in their own collections, if there is in fact such demand.

Why Not Just Donate Instead?

Of course an even better option is if the patron opts to donate such materials to the library outright instead, so that the library's ownership is uncontested and the library is solely responsible for anything that happens to the item or items. In fact, many patrons are often looking for opportunities such as this to perform a simple act of philanthropy. Most public libraries actively solicit book and other media donations, but not all libraries will accept nontraditional materials such as toys and games. Consider, however, how many households are left with myriad games and other collectibles once kids move away to college. Patrons may consider donating these items to a thrift store or selling them at a yard sale, but why not encourage them to bring these things to the library first along with their used books, CDs, DVDs, and LP records instead? Incidentally, this is a great way for your MakerSpace to pick up electronic toys in various states of repair/disrepair for "dissection" and pounds of building toys, such as Capsela or LEGO bricks!

If your library has a regular used book sale, consider adding your call for games and gaming materials to this event, or holding your own separate drive if not. Just be prepared! Once you've made it clear that you accept these sorts of donations, you may end up opening the floodgates to your community. As with book donations, be sure that your donation terms for gaming materials are clear: that all donations will be evaluated in terms of quality and completeness and there is no guarantee that you will make items donated part of the games collection. After all, there are only so many copies of Trivial Pursuit that you can reasonably add to your gaming shelves.

⊚ You Wouldn't Download a Game, or Would You?

Finally we come to the second-oldest way to add games to your library's collection: steal them! Mind you, I'm only being half-facetious because as it turns out games do not enjoy the same level of copyright protection that other more traditional library materials enjoy. For example, while you might be able to trademark the specific names and images associated with a board game, you cannot do the same for the game's rules or gameplay—nor may you copyright these things. What this means is that, in the case of some board games, you are well within your legal rights to make your own version of the game, as long as you don't reproduce the components of the game that are protected by copyright. If this sounds like an awesome excuse for a MakerSpace project, you are exactly right, and creating your own games is something that we'll cover in greater detail in chapter 11.

That being said, however, there is also a growing genre of what are called "print and play" games, which are free games available online in PDF format for anyone to download, print, and play. For the price of some cardstock paper, some toner, and a laminator, you can have access to a surprising amount of quality gaming content. Cheapass Games maintains a list of their free offerings, including some new games in beta test, at cheapass.com/free-games; Good Little Games (www.goodlittlegames.co.uk/) is a free print-and-play game company that underwrites its development costs using the creative crowdfunding platform Patreon; and BoardGameGeek.com maintains what it calls a canonical list of free print-and-play games at the following URL: boardgamegeek.com/boardgamecategory/1120/print-play.

Free video games are harder to come by for console games, but free computer games can be found in a variety of different places—we'll provide a short list of quality free video games in chapter 7. In the case of console and classic arcade games, however, you may also want to consider running an emulator, which not only is free but also allows you access to a large quantity of classic and retro titles as well. We will discuss emulators at greater length again when we talk about video games in chapter 7 and again in the context of MakerSpace gaming projects in chapter 11. In the meantime, I hope I've made it clear that there are many options available to the would-be gaming librarian in establishing your core collection of games. Given the circumstances, any of the strategies mentioned above may be valid for your library, whether you have a significant amount of budget discretion and funds for your project or whether you are trying to acquire as much as you possibly can for free.

⊚ Key Points

- No matter what your library's budget is, you should be able to come up with a games acquisition plan to get you started.
- Traditional library vendors are increasingly offering games and gaming materials, but there is still no substitute for good relationships with local businesses.
- It's easy to find quality used games at thrift shops, at estate sales, and in the clearance section of major stores.
- Consider asking your community to donate games as well as books for seasonal/annual book sales and other material drives.

CHAPTER 4

How to Circulate Your Library Gaming Collection and Live to Tell the Tale

---

IN THIS CHAPTER

▷ γνῶθι σεαυτόν: Know Yourself

▷ Publicity, or Getting the Word Out

▷ Support, or Eating Your Own Gaming Dog Food

▷ Collection Integrity, or What's the Fine for Losing a Meeple?

---

⑥ γνῶθι σεαυτόν: Know Yourself

LET US BEGIN THIS CHAPTER by reiterating that there are many ways to set up your library gaming collection. A configuration that works perfectly in one library may not work at all in another institution, and solutions to problems that seem to be universal may in fact not be universally applicable. Therefore the most important thing you can do as a gaming librarian is first and foremost to know your own library, understand your community, and anticipate the needs of your patrons, staff, and other stakeholders—or, as the Delphic Oracle so succinctly exhorted: "γνῶθι σεαυτόν," or know thyself. That being said, there is a wealth of libraries currently experimenting with various levels of implementing library gaming collections, which means there is ample opportunity to learn from others' successes and failures before venturing into unfamiliar territory. This leads us to my second exhortation: always leverage the experience of your colleagues when looking to implement new library services. Every library is its own unique incubator for innovation, but if you can identify a peer group of institutions similar in size and focus as your own, make sure you at the very least see if they've attempted to implement similar services in the past.

At the risk of getting up on my soapbox and lecturing my fellow librarians, let me also emphasize the importance of sharing your successes and failures with the library community as widely and as often as possible. I know that the last thing librarians have on their hands is free time, which means unless there is a built-in institutional mandate to assess a new library collection or service—or a personal requirement to publish or present in order to secure tenure or achieve promotion on the job—the chances of having a moment to pause and reflect are slim to none. Based on my own anecdotal evidence of working in libraries over the past twenty years, most new services are launched perhaps with some local fanfare, but very quickly the institution moves on to the next priority or big project and the opportunity to divine any broader insights when the implementation process is still fresh in everyone's mind is lost. Consider, however, how useful this information might be to other librarians if shared in the proper forum. At best such knowledge and experience could prove inspirational to other libraries considering following suit with adding a similar collection or service, but even highlighting the challenges and difficulties that arose during the implementation process can be of enormous assistance in helping other librarians anticipate their own potential roadblocks along the way.

This brings us to part two of my soapbox, and that's not being afraid to talk about failure. I understand that this is a difficult topic for many of us to approach, for fear of looking incompetent or incapable of performing one's basic job responsibilities, but it is true that there is no greater teacher than failure itself. We may be able to inspire one another by gathering together and crowing about our successes, but when we come together to talk about things that did not go as expected, we find that our audience is suddenly a little more attentive, a little more receptive . . . even on the edge of their seats. Yes, there's a bit of *schadenfreude* at work here—i.e., better that it happened to your library than to mine—and the not-so-secret pleasure of watching other librarians wrestle with their own demons, but there is also the understanding that talking about failure in our circles is still rare and that as a result the wisdom gleaned from such revelations is still rather precious. But let's face it: as a profession we don't have the time, resources, or energy not to learn from each other's mistakes, so it is incumbent upon us to be willing to share about both our successes and our failures. The most important kind of self-knowledge is understanding one's own limitations or shortcomings, not so that this information can be used to shut down innovation or prevent one from trying new things, but so that one is able to endeavor to innovate armed with the best possible foreknowledge of what might go wrong and how to overcome any potential obstacles on the path to implementation.

So much for the pep talk. Let us return to the beginning of the chapter, where I mentioned that there is a continuum of potential solutions to the problem of adding a circulating gaming collection to your library. For the sake of simplicity we are going to reduce this continuum to several discrete options, presented in ascending levels of complexity that your library will have to account for:

1. Noncirculating games collection. This is the simplest form, whereby your games are not accounted for or tracked in your ILS, nor are they discoverable in your catalog. Many libraries that have dipped their toes into supporting games but have not necessarily embraced it programmatically maintain a selection of games available for in-library use only. Most of the time these games will live at the library circulation desk or be gathered and stored in one particular place (say, a cabinet adjacent to some publicly available tables or desks). Even if a library does not offer

games in this manner, they probably already do something similar with things like puzzles or other similar materials, so it can be a relative easy transition to "add" games to one's available offerings.

2. Informal games collection. This is a step up from the simplest option, whereby your games are still not accounted for or tracked in your ILS (nor are they discoverable in your catalog), but they can be borrowed and circulated informally via some form of manual check-in/check-out. If your library already has an existing gaming group or meetup, you could leverage this group to help serve as custodians for this collection. Obviously your main problems here are visibility and access. If the collection only ends up serving the needs of a gaming group and not the larger library community, is this an efficient or equitable use of library funds? Also, with a less formal system of circulation, one is relying on something akin to the honor system to ensure that games are returned intact and in a timely manner—again, this may work just fine with a smaller group of gamers who may already know one another, but does this kind of system scale if you open it up to your entire library community?

3. Mediated games collection. In this option the games have been barcoded and cataloged by the library and are therefore discoverable to some extent in the ILS. However, instead of just sitting open on the shelves somewhere in your library, this collection lives where access can be mediated by a certain group who has been specially trained to circulate games in the library and who can anticipate any problems that may arise during the check-in and check-out processes. Also, these staff are ideally knowledgeable about the games themselves and can offer basic advice on how to play them. This option works well if you already have an established group or place within your library dedicated to experiential learning—for example, a library MakerSpace—as your patrons are already "programmed" to expect to find such items and such expertise available in this space. The experiential learning staff can also help demystify games that might be unfamiliar to a traditional audience, such as the new genre of Eurogames featuring titles like Catan, Agricola, or Carcassonne. While there can be a danger of locking up too many resources in a programmed space, especially if that space is not open and welcoming to all of your patron demographics, the library's extra investment in these resources in terms of expertise and training can help introduce them to a wider audience.

4. Unmediated games collection. There is a certain attraction to not treating games any differently than any other category of library material. Why not simply barcode, catalog them, and put them on the shelf? Although this option appears on the surface to be simpler than the other two configurations we have already explored, there is actually a great deal of complexity under the surface that your library will have to deal with in terms of training and support. Also, this option assumes that your patrons, staff, and other library stakeholders will know what to do with a gaming collection if it suddenly materializes in your library stacks. This may very well be the case if you are working at a library with an established "Library of Things"–type of collection, but if not you may want to make sure that you have a plan to properly introduce this exciting new collection to your community.

While I'm sure there are many other configurations currently deployed out there in the library world, most of them will end up being some kind of variation on the four basic scenarios I have outlined above.

🌀 Publicity, or Getting the Word Out

Your patrons have limited bandwidth for library news and announcements, so getting the word out about new library gaming collections, services, and activities can be challenging to say the least. While we will explore strategies for connecting with your local gaming community and promoting gaming events at your library in the next chapter, it is useful to consider how you will market the launch of the gaming collection itself as well. Again, if your library already had a successful track record in offering and circulating "nontraditional" items—which can range from anything from ukuleles to bicycle pumps—then you already have an obvious point of reference that you can leverage to this end. If gaming items are your first foray into supporting a circulating "Library of Things," however, then you should make sure you spend at least as much time figuring out how you are going to communicate these new acquisitions as you do actually acquiring the items themselves. Be sure to work with your communications staff to coordinate publicity using your library's established methods of pushing out information to your patrons, considering the importance of lead times if you are taking advantage of printed and mailed channels of communication. In the next chapter, we will look at specific social media strategies for engaging the gamers in your library community, but it is important to bear in mind that the average gamer or gaming-interested patron tends to be more technologically savvy than your ordinary library patron and thus more "reachable" via newer forms of media, such as Facebook Groups, Meetup, or even Reddit.

Consider also how you will make your gaming collection discoverable, both physically as well as in a bibliographic sense. If your library has displays to feature new books or other library materials, perhaps showcasing the more attractive games in your collection might be a good use of that shelf space. If you really want to get creative (and you and your library can afford an additional copy of a game), a layout display of a featured board game as if in the middle of play can be a dramatic way to highlight the new collection. You may also want to think about scheduling regular "Learn to Play" events, which can be coordinated with your acquisitions of new games—not only do such events help shine a spotlight on your new library gaming collection, but they also provide a safe point of entry for people curious about certain types of games but who don't know where to learn more about them or even how to get started.

🌀 Support, or Eating Your Own Gaming Dog Food

We've talked a bit about the importance of gaming literacy and overcoming the roadblocks among various library stakeholders about the social or moral usefulness of games, but let's revisit this topic once more through a different perspective. There's a great term in marketing called "dogfooding," or eating your own dog food. The idea behind it is that if the people in a company actually use the products they are trying to sell—i.e., feeding their company's brand of dog food to their own dogs—then they will be more knowledgeable and passionate about said products. While this isn't exactly a new concept for librarians, as we have been dogfooding the books in our own collections since time immemorial, one of the challenges of offering new kinds of circulating materials is that our own personal familiarity with them might be variable, and hence our enthusiasm not as keen as it is for more traditional forms of readers' advisory.

This is a topic I've written about before—in *Wearable Technology: Smart Watches to Google Glass*, I argue that in order for librarians and library staff to become effective mediators between their patrons and new forms of technology, they must feel empowered to explore and become acquainted with these technologies as part of their general training:

> In general, the more knowledgeable your library staff is about new technology, the better interpreters they can be of these devices for your library patrons. It is therefore just as important to hold demonstrations and other outreach sessions internally as well as externally. Your goal in offering a loanable wearable technology program is not to impress yourself, your community, and your peers with being "cutting edge" in your embrace of the Next Big Thing, but to provide the most conducive environment to your patrons as they experiment with and explore these new technologies. For all of its flashiness, always remember that technology is only as useful as your library's ability to support it. (Bruno 2015, 91)

Does this mean every library staff member now has to become a gamer as well? Of course not. But we must recognize that gaming literacy will increasingly become a more and more important part of the overall concept of media literacy, and while we don't expect librarians to be experts on all forms of knowledge, we do at the very least ask that they know enough to steer our patrons in the right direction when they come to us with their questions and other informational needs. To be fair, this concept can provoke some interesting forms of pushback—not just from staff who may not be gamer-friendly but also from administrators and other stakeholders wary of committing library resources to "playing games." Play as a legitimate form of media literacy is a relatively new concept, and unfortunately many people still consider games and gaming to be intrinsically less important than other library collections or other activities.

How do we overcome this stigma? Familiarity is the most important thing. Consider having a facilitated "games day" for your next library staff day, where staff can get hands-on experience playing various forms of games that the library collects—from puzzles and board games to video games and role-playing games. Although we are supposedly in a board gaming renaissance, for many people their last board game experience was playing Monopoly with their family over the holidays or Candy Land with their children. Showing them that there is a new world of games available corresponding to practically any interest under the sun is a great way to get people to reconsider their attitudes toward gaming. Similarly, for video games one can choose to introduce gaming platforms with proven track records of engaging demographics outside of the expected crowd of young males. For example, showing off video games like the Wii U or Nintendo Switch can emphasize the universal appeal of casual play. Although libraries now offer many different kinds of "dog food" (cat food? fish food? bird food?), the belief that a library should champion the literacies it cultivates remains unchanged; if gaming literacy is to enjoy the same level of importance as reading and other forms of media literacy, it will in no small part be due to our efforts to help mainstream gaming within our library communities.

Collection Integrity, or What's the Fine for Losing a Meeple?

One of the chief objections raised whenever a library considers collecting and circulating games is: how will we ensure that our patrons won't lose any pieces when they borrow them? The simplest answer is: you can't. Make your peace with this now. If you circulate games, things will get lost, just as surely as patrons who borrow DVDs of television series will inevitably misplace disc 5 in a six-disc set. If you circulate video games, expect components like controllers or cables to go missing; if you circulate board games, expect your patrons to return them missing a meeple here or a plastic train there. Maybe their dog will eat the custom dice that came with the game, or perhaps their toddler will squash a little plastic game piece or draw in crayon on the board. Whatever it is you can imagine, it will probably happen, so by all means let this disaster scenario play out to its logical conclusion in your head and come back to me when you've finished. Now that you've imagined how things can go wrong, let's try to anticipate these disasters and see if we can't head them off through a combination of proper policies and procedures, some cleverness on our part, and most importantly the careful management of both the expectations of our patrons and those of our own institutional culture.

Obviously we are probably going to want to adopt different approaches for analog and electronic games. Losing a handful of board game components, while frustrating, is relatively easily remedied and not going to prevent the next patron from using the materials; whereas if a patron loses a cable or controller for a video game system, the item may well be unplayable until a replacement can be procured. A common solution to the problem of circulating items with critical electronic components is to barcode each piece separately and check out each piece as part of the circulation transaction. Not only does this provide a check at the beginning of the transaction to ensure that all of the pieces are in fact present at the time of checkout, but it also walks the patron through an inventory of the library material's essential component parts. Of course it also provides real leverage over the patron should they fail to return the individual components, as each one is represented by an actionable circulation record in the system.

Although some libraries have followed a similar system for board game components, it is more likely that only the game as a whole will be barcoded in the ILS for circulation. The most notable exception to this would be a game that featured an extremely expensive component, such as an electronic accessory or something that provided a critical in-game function. Interestingly enough, this is a bottleneck that game creators themselves have begun to identify and remedy by coding companion apps for smartphones or tablets that provide the desired electronic functionality without having to include an expensive piece of custom hardware that can break or be lost at some point. At any rate, instead of barcoding and circulating the internal components separately, most board games will contain a packing list—either one originally provided by the manufacturer or one specifically created by the library—that library staff can review upon checkout and check against when the item is returned.

Here is where your library must make a decision: how much time are you going to invest in the circulation process itself? While it is a relatively easy affair to count out all of the game pieces in a chess set, modern board games can have hundreds or even thousands of small pieces, making each circulation transaction a time-consuming and frustrating process for staff and patrons alike. Indeed, many libraries that have insisted upon checking the inventory of game boxes at one or both points in the circulation transaction have done so to the grumbling of their library staff, who are often saddled with the tedious task of accounting for all those little pieces of wood, plastic, and paper. This can also impact the normal circulation workflow, especially if you have decided that all library gaming materials should be checked in and out through the same service point as books and other library media—not surprisingly, this is one of the reasons why many libraries opt for a mediated or semi-mediated approach for library materials requiring a complex circulation transaction or series of transactions. Certainly it is a point in favor for circulating gaming materials through a MakerSpace or some other similar such service point.

Another workflow alternative is to stage returns of gaming materials on an intermediate shelf, where they can be checked in more thoroughly later in the day when the circulation desk isn't as busy. One potential downside with such a system is that the games do not circulate back to being available immediately but must pass through an additional bottleneck before another patron can make use of them. Another potential problem is that something might happen to the gaming materials while awaiting full inspection, meaning that the patron could be left being held responsible for missing materials or components that they returned in good faith. While this is probably more of an outlier situation than a general cause for concern, it does at the very least highlight the need to locate your staging area in a place that is reasonably secure.

Another method of quickly assessing the completeness of board games when they circulate is to use a gram scale. This is a method that is quite popular at gaming conventions that feature collections of board games that can be played at the conference venue. (It is also used by other organizations that loan materials such as LEGO kits, as a gram scale can identify as little as one brick being missing from the kit. At the Westport Library, we successfully adapted using gram scales to loan out our MakerSpace kits for Little Bits and LEGO Mindstorms.) Instead of requiring staff to ensure all of the gaming components are visually accounted for, a quick weigh-in at checkout and again at check-in can serve the same purpose in a much more efficient manner. If the item does not match the expected weight at either end of the process, only then would the staff member initiate a more thorough accounting of game components.

With the question of how to hold patrons accountable having been answered, we must now decide exactly how much to hold patrons accountable if they should happen to break or lose any game components. Insofar as we've already found a workflow solution to the problem of expensive or critical electronic components, I think holding a patron accountable for the amount of money necessary to replace these items is the most prudent course of action, with the following exception: if the component in question is known to be unusually fragile or easy to lose or break, then perhaps some leniency could or should be extended to the patron for such a "known issue." Otherwise these little costs to keep one's gaming collection operational can quickly add up and impact your library's ability to acquire new materials.

In the case of board games, however, I would caution against holding patrons fiscally responsible for replacing lost components. Not only are many of them available now from the game manufacturer at a nominal cost or even for free, but many plastic or wooden components can now be replaced through printing or carving your own. In fact, reproducing missing or lost gaming components can very easily become a MakerSpace activity, where your staff or volunteers could locate the components on Thingiverse or similar 3-D printing template search engines or scan and/or design their own replacements. Gone are the days when one missing piece would doom a board game to the trashcan—now you can find PDF files for missing rules and instructions, as well as printable PDFs for cards and other paper or cardboard gaming components that are essential for play. Also, except in the rare cases of vintage collectible board games such as Fireball Island, even in the worst case scenario you can usually find another copy of the game on eBay or Amazon that can be harvested for spare parts, if nothing else. Your MakerSpace staff will have their interest piqued by the challenge, and your patron will be thankful for not having to pay to replace an entire board game just for the sake of a few missing components.

⊚ Key Points

- Before you start to implement a library gaming program, it is important to understand your library, your community, and your work culture and set realistic goals accordingly.
- Creating a gamer-friendly library means taking the time and care to train gamer-friendly staff—not just the staff running the programs but the public service staff who will support it and help circulate gaming materials to your public.
- There are several different models for circulating gaming materials, ranging from treating them just like books to keeping them in house as a kind of playable special collection.
- Consider alternatives to replacement fees for missing components—i.e., can your MakerSpace help print lost pieces?

⊚ Reference

Bruno, Tom. 2015. *Wearable Technology: Smart Watches to Google Glass.* Library Technology Essentials Series, no. 1. Lanham, MD: Rowman & Littlefield.

CHAPTER 5

How to Create, Evaluate, and Assess Gaming Programming for Your Library

IN THIS CHAPTER

▷ Making It Look Easy Is Hard Work

▷ The Importance of Planning Ahead—and Not So Much

▷ Thematic Planning and the Year Ahead

▷ Who Are Your Gaming Programming Stakeholders?

▷ Let's Get Granular

▷ Other Gaming Programming Cycles: Weekly and Monthly Activities

▷ There's Nothing Wrong with Starting Small

▷ Evaluation and Assessment by the Numbers

▷ Going Beyond the Numbers

▷ Conclusion: Now That Wasn't So Hard, Was It?

Making It Look Easy Is Hard Work

IN THIS CHAPTER, WE'RE GOING TO LOOK at how to plan your library gaming programming. This is no small task, as by now you must be aware that gaming potentially touches on many different departments and stakeholders in your library. In order to successfully plan any kind of gaming activities or events at the library, you're going to need to include these people and their own scheduled programming into your overall planning process. Also, you will want to craft your gaming programming in such a way that you are not overwhelming or underwhelming your potential audience coming out of the gate, so that managing the expectations of both your community and your colleagues is on your mind, as well as incorporating a plan to evaluate and assess your gaming efforts from the moment your first board game is ready to be loaned out. Finally, you want this process, as complex and demanding though it may be, to look as casual and unaffected as possible, as despite all of your efforts you want your library gaming programming to come across as something that is exciting, spontaneous, and fun.

No problem at all, right? Let's get started.

◎ The Importance of Planning Ahead—And Not So Much

Here's a not-so-secret secret—libraries have a difficult time planning ahead. Okay, if you've worked as a librarian for even a year or so, this probably isn't exactly a revelation to you, but it's something you definitely want to keep in mind as you sit down to craft your first cycles of schedules for library programming. Libraries tend either to underprogram or overprogram for a given genre of activity. In the case of underprogramming, the library has failed to include enough recurring events so as to generate a sense of momentum or buzz around that theme, with the result that the programming feels disjointed and disconnected and not part of a consistent, thematic whole. Overprogramming, on the other hand, is almost even more dangerous, as it can sap the attention span of your patrons and the enthusiasm of your library staff and volunteers. It can also severely restrict your library's breathing room to either try new things or adjust its offerings on a short- or medium-term basis in order to accommodate new trends or items of topical interest that may be engaging now but not necessarily six months from now.

Those pesky Greeks have another phrase that is particularly relevant to what we are trying to accomplish here: μηδὲν ἄγαν, or nothing in excess. Successful library programming in general should look ahead so as to create a coherent framework that signals to both your patrons and your staff the shape of things to come, while at the same permitting enough looseness or flexibility to allow your community to experiment, try new things, and grow. It's a kind of tightrope walking, to be sure, and especially at the outset it might be challenging to strike the right balance, as doubtless you and your staff will be chock full of ideas you just can't wait to get started. However, try to keep this guiding principle in mind from the very beginning and it will serve you well.

◎ Thematic Planning and the Year Ahead

If your library is like most public libraries, your planning cycle is probably looking four to six months ahead except during extraordinary circumstances like strategic planning or some other kind of broader assessment. While this isn't a bad time frame for implementing and executing actual ideas, you may find it useful to think ahead in broader, more thematic terms. For example, are there any recurring annual events around which you'd like to plan your gaming programming? Perhaps you'd like to offer programming for International Games @ Your Library Day, an all-day event in November sponsored by the American Library Association, or International Tabletop Day, a similar event in April that has been promoted by Geek & Sundry, a commercial YouTube channel and multimedia production company geared toward the gaming demographic. Does your library offer stress-relieving programming for high school and college students at the end of each school semester? These might be excellent days around which to plan some of your gaming programming. Sit down with your annual calendar and block out the parts of the year when you know you want to be doing something on a recurring annual basis.

After this you want to do the same thing with the entire year, only this time looking at nonrecurring events coming up that may be of particular library interest. For example, will the Olympics be held this year or some other sports tournament like the FIFA World Cup? Are there any blockbuster movies set to be released in the upcoming year that could be tied into some of your gaming programming (*Star Wars* is an example that comes immediately to mind)? What about regional or local events going on in your extended community? Perhaps your town is celebrating a historic anniversary this year commemorating someone or something around which you could plan. The possibilities here are almost limitless. Mind you, at this stage of the programming process, it is not even necessary to have a fully realized event or implementation plan. The advantage of thematic planning is that you have looked ahead a sufficient distance and identified the major themes you want to highlight with your library gaming programming and activities.

A very rough thematic plan might look something like this:

- January: Midterm Stress Busters/Mario Kart and Smash Bros. Tournament
- February: Board Games for Two, Valentine's Day
- March: From Agricola to Starview Valley, Games Featuring Gardening, Agriculture, and Growing
- April: International Tabletop Day
- May: Final Exam Stress Busters/Magic: The Gathering, Pokémon, and other collectible card games
- June: World Cup 2018 in Russia
- July: Summer Reading Challenge/Independence Day Revolutionary War mini painting and war-gaming diorama crafting
- August: Gaming on Vacation: Board Games That Travel Well
- September: Back to School Gaming Takeover
- October: Halloween Activities and Games
- November: International Games @ Your Library Day
- December: *Star Wars*! Painting miniatures, playing X-Wing, and other fun stuff to celebrate the latest movie in the franchise.

Who Are Your Gaming Programming Stakeholders?

This kind of programming brainstorming is best done in a group setting. Does your library already have a programming librarian or library staff whose primary responsibility is library programming as a whole? Be sure to invite this person or group at the very least, but ideally you want as broad a group of potential stakeholders as your organization can spare for this kind of planning activity. For example, having a children's or teen librarian in the group can help you avoid counterprogramming one another around similar recurring or nonrecurring events—say, for instance, the release of a new YA genre book like *Harry Potter*. It might also be useful to include members of your other public services branches, such as reference or circulation, as they might be able to provide some anecdotal insight into what patrons might want to see in their gaming programming. Do you have a communications department? Be sure to include them, or at least be sure to keep them in the loop even if they can't attend these meetings regularly. Don't forget your community as well. If you already have an established gaming group that you work with regularly, such as a local Meetup, then consider inviting them as well. How better to plan community-driven programming than by making the community part of the planning process!

Let's Get Granular

Once you have drafted your thematic plan for the upcoming year, it's time to start filling out the event-planning process. This is where your normal four- to six-month event horizon for library programing usually comes into play: inviting experts and speakers; reserving/securing space for the event; purchasing games and other gaming-related materials for the event; scheduling staffing and anticipating any special needs such as café service, unusually late staffing, janitorial, or security; starting the print and online publicity process (which we have already covered in the previous chapter). There are many wheels within wheels for this kind of planning, so if you have anyone with strong organizational skills or experience in project management, be sure to take advantage of his or her expertise if at all possible or work to build these talents as part of your own skill set.

Other Gaming Programming Cycles: Weekly and Monthly Activities

In addition to the year-long cycle of recurring and nonrecurring programming, there will be gaming events that will recur on a monthly or even weekly basis. For example, many libraries have a weekly chess club that will meet on a particular afternoon or evening every week. Similarly, libraries that host gaming community meetups may do so on a semi-regular or regular basis, some meeting monthly while others meet weekly or every other week. You should consider building some consistent events of your own into this structure. Perhaps you can have an open play session one evening every week, where people can come and play from a selection of board games or a featured role-playing game (if your Gamemaster and players don't mind playing out in the open, of course!), or an ongoing "drop-in" video game night. Not every one of these weekly events needs to be a breakaway hit in its own right, but what they do in the aggregate is help advertise that you're changing the everyday culture of your library to something that is gamer-positive/gamer-friendly.

In fact, the more informal you can make these events feel when you get down to the weekly or biweekly level, the more spontaneous and fun they will seem to those who are involved. It's not that there's anything wrong with preparation, and the fact that we're even talking about this as part of the planning process should show you that it's more about the seeming than the actuality of things. Gaming is something that is spur-of-the-moment and exciting, so you want to try to craft some regular recurring events in your library gaming calendar that capture this sense of spontaneity: "Oh, wow—are they playing Fireball Island? I haven't seen that game in years. Let's go check it out!"

◎ There's Nothing Wrong with Starting Small

Especially when you're starting out, there's nothing wrong with making your gaming programming seem like one of the library's best-kept secrets. This will allow you to manage your patrons' expectations as your community grows beyond a table of gamers and onlookers to a room full of people who want in on the fun—a transition that will require a decent assessment and growth plan in order to anticipate. For the remainder of this chapter, we will take a closer look about how to evaluate and assess your library gaming programming and, perhaps most importantly, how to make this assessment process actionable so that it results in the additional resources you'll need—both in terms of materials and people—in order to grow your programs and activities.

◎ Evaluation and Assessment by the Numbers

One of the simplest ways to evaluate the effectiveness of your gaming programming efforts is to look at your library's statistics. These should include:

- Circulation statistics for any games that have been added to the library collection. Are you seeing any trends after three months, in other words, any games that are more popular than others? If you are seeing evidence of some games not circulating at all, perhaps you should consider highlighting them at a future open gaming or "learn to play" session or blogging about them online on your library website if you have a space for that kind of communication.
- If you are seeing any breakaway hits, this may be a good time to add additional circulating copies of these games or collect "play-alikes" or games that are similar in style and play to the ones that are currently flying off the shelves. For example, if Ticket to Ride is proving to be an extremely popular circulating game, you may want to think about purchasing copies of Ticket to Ride: Europe or Ticket to Ride: Rails to Sails as well. Consider weeding or donating games that aren't circulating after a year of trial and error, so as not to clutter your shelf with games that don't capture your community's interest.
- Circulation statistics for sections of your collection that are related to gaming, including books, ebooks, comics and graphic novels, and movies and television. Are you seeing upticks in circulation in these parts of your collection? If you can show that they correlate to certain gaming-related programs and activities, that can help you build a positive narrative of gaming drawing in hidden demographics who will in turn use other library materials and services once they are in the building.
- If you do manage to show some promising data in this regard, consider making them available to your peers either by sharing them via social media or at a conference or publishing them with a reputable library science journal, as these are exactly the kind of hard data that administrators look for when making decisions about whether to support these kinds of programs.
- Also, this is an opportunity for you to work more closely with the librarians responsible for the impacted parts of the collection. If certain kinds of games and gaming activities resulted in increased library use and circulation, then how do you want to continue to enable this trend? Sitting down with the selectors may give you additional library gaming programming ideas as well.

- Attendance numbers for your library gaming programs. Be sure to try and get an accurate count of attendees for all of your programming, especially the "informal" weekly and biweekly events that represent the bulk of your activities. Again, just because you want things to feel informal doesn't mean that you shouldn't put the same amount of effort into planning, executing, and assessing it that you do for any other kind of library programming!

- Are you noticing any interesting trends at the three-month mark? For example, if you have programming that is already growing beyond capacity, consider adding additional sessions or expanding the venue from a table to a room. Conversely, if you notice that certain programs are not getting the attendance numbers that you'd thought they would, try and ask yourself why. Are there external factors that may be impacting your potential attendance—for example, did you try and plan a teen gaming activity during a busy week for your local schools, was the weather a factor that day, or are you accidentally counterprogramming another institution nearby offering similar events, be it another library, a bookstore or hobby shop, a teen center, or your friendly local game store?

Remember that not every library program needs to be a sold-out event. Some kinds of library programs will attract a smaller but more reliable demographic, and serving this part of your community is just as important as delivering standing-room-only author talks. Instead of cancelling these seemingly underperforming programs as a knee-jerk reaction, track their progress over several months and see whether the attendance is hit and miss or steady—in the case of the latter, you may want to think about keeping the program and the demographic that it's serving if you have the resources to sustain it.

Going Beyond the Numbers

It is just as important to have qualitative data as it is to have quantitative data when evaluating and assessing your programming. Numbers can tell you a lot, but they can't capture the entire story. Many public libraries include a written evaluation/assessment form as part of any programming they sponsor—although this is no guarantee that everyone in attendance will fill one out, if you commit to making them a regular feature of your library programming, your patrons will eventually come to expect it. To that end, consider ditching the long-form surveys in favor of one that is short and sweet and gets to the point:

1. What program did you attend?
2. How did you learn about this program (multiple choice)?
3. Have you used the library prior to this event (Y/N)?
4. How would you rate this program (scale of 1 to 5)?
5. In the future, what new programming would you like to see at your library?

It is tempting to try and gather additional demographic data with these forms—for example, are you a resident of this town, do you have a library card, and so on. I would recommend strongly against weighing down your form with these kinds of questions on a regular basis. If you wish to drill down deeper with a more involved survey, consider not attaching it to any one given library program and also think about incentivizing participation, perhaps with a raffle or giveaway, but the basic rule of thumb is that the shorter the after-program survey, the more likely you are to have people complete it.

In addition to any written feedback forms, when you host library gaming events, try to gather as much anecdotal feedback as you can, and encourage other participating staff and volunteers to do the same. Try to meet with participating staff as soon as possible after the event to debrief and see what the positive and negative takeaways were from the attendee's perspective. This kind of debrief is actually a great thing to incorporate into your programming stakeholders' group meetings (as mentioned earlier in the chapter), as are the written evaluation forms, as including and discussing patron feedback helps ensure that the data you're gathering remain actionable and timely, as they become part of the active library game programming planning cycle and not just crammed into a filing cabinet somewhere.

⑥ Conclusion—Now That Wasn't So Hard, Was It?

In reality committing oneself to a programmatic planning, evaluation/assessment, and growth model such as this is an extraordinarily difficult thing to do. Many libraries attempt this level of planning or aspire to it as an ideal, but it is so tempting to let a meeting slide here and a deadline go there that the entire structure can threaten to unravel very quickly if you don't maintain your resolve. While I am by no means whatsoever a fan of meetings for meetings' sake, having seen this kind of planning structure work extremely effectively in many different library settings, I must say that cross-functional stakeholders groups such as the one mentioned above for library programming is worth sacrificing that hour and change every two weeks in your work calendar. These groups easily pay that time back and then some in terms of the ideas generated, the workflow sustained, and the potential pitfalls identified and dispatched weeks or even months before they threaten to become a problem.

⑥ Key Points

- Successful library gaming programming should be holistically integrated with the rest of your library programming from the start.
- Thematic programming is a great way to plan ahead using large brush strokes and excellent inspiration for other stakeholders to respond with programming addressing that theme as well.
- The best daily library gaming program feels spontaneous and fun—allow your staff time and resources to experiment to find games and gaming activities that really resonate with your community.
- Be sure to take your assessment beyond mere numbers by looking for the hidden stories in the statistics, like correlations between gaming programs and library circulation rates.
- Surveys can be an effective way to gauge patron interest if you can keep them short and sweet.
- Not all programs need to be grand slams—your library programming portfolio should be able to accommodate smaller but faithful demographics from your community (this is especially true for gamers!).

CHAPTER 6

How to Implement Board Game Programming in Your Library

IN THIS CHAPTER

▷ You've Gotten to Yes—Now What?

▷ Board Game Clubs as Programming and Community

▷ Whose Turn Is It, Anyway?

▷ Outfitting Your Gaming Club

▷ Beyond Gaming Club: "Learn to Play" Events and Other Forms of Outreach

▷ Themed Game Events and Local Tournaments

▷ "Legacy" Games and the Library: Like Oil and Water or PB and J?

▷ Binge-Play with Us: Legacy Games as Library Event

▷ Sponsoring Local Gaming Tournaments @ Your Library

▷ Winning Is the Easy Part: How to Keep Score for Tournament Rankings

▷ To the Victors: Prizes for Your Library Gaming Tournament

▷ Other Special Gaming Events @ Your Library—Enter Wil Wheaton

▷ Don't Forget the Librarians!

▷ Board Game Events and Thematic Programming

▷ War (Gaming): What Is It Good For?

▷ Other Thematic Gaming Programming @ Your Library

▷ Conclusion: You Will Never Be Bored with Board Games

Playing Catan using the Pennsylvania/New Jersey Map.

You've Gotten to Yes—Now What?

SO FAR IN THIS BOOK you have learned how to make the case for gaming in your library, how to acquire games and gaming materials, and how to catalog, barcode, and circulate them as part of your collection. You have also learned the basics of mapping out gaming programming in your library and how to promote your recurring and special gaming events using traditional media, social media, and other unorthodox but nevertheless effective alternative means of communication. Now we will cover how to implement library gaming programming specifically by game genre, showing you how to brainstorm, plan, prepare, and run each kind of event at your library. With board games being one of the "safest" points of entry for introducing gaming programming in the library, let us begin with board gaming programming—subsequent chapters will address collective card games, video games, role-playing games, virtual worlds, augmented reality games, and large-scale "takeover" events such as miniature golf and escape rooms.

Board Game Clubs as Programming and Community

The simplest yet one of the most effective ways to initiate board gaming programming at your library is to start a board game club. You can accomplish this either by starting your own with a library staff member or volunteer in charge of the event, or you could reach out to your local gaming community and see if anyone would be interested in partnering with the library on sponsoring a regular meeting. One way to reach out to the gaming community for this purpose is to contact your friendly local game store (or FLGS, and yes—this is a real, albeit unofficial term), which is usually a clearinghouse for gaming groups in need of players and space; also, your FLGS itself might consider partnering or sponsoring not only a regular gaming club but other gaming events at your library. In chapter 3 we discussed how you can approach your FLGS and other game vendors for discounted or even free gaming materials for your library—approaching these groups as potential community partners with a stake in your library programming helps make the relationship more reciprocal in nature.

Another way to enlist the local gaming community is through social media, such as Facebook Groups or Meetup. Although there are dedicated "find a game/gamer" online services that exist out there, such as FindGamers.us, NearbyGamers.com, or the /r/lfg ("Looking For Group") subreddit on Reddit, Meetup is by far the most comprehensive online list of board gaming enthusiasts, with more than 400,000 members across almost 1,500 gaming groups. Depending on how your library does its public relations and communications, your library may already be using Meetup, which makes it easier and somewhat less awkward for you to approach a group using the platform in an official capacity as library staff; if your library is not already using Meetup, however, anecdotally I've found that creating a personal account on Meetup for reaching out to and communicating with groups about library events is also welcomed—in fact, many groups are thrilled that a librarian has gone to all of the trouble of meeting them halfway on their preferred platform!

⌾ Whose Turn Is It, Anyway?

Whether you enlist your community or start from scratch, the first thing you must do is make sure that your board game club has a dedicated library staff member or volunteer who can regularly attend club meetings. This is important not just for the sake of basic administrative oversight but for several reasons:

1. The staff member/volunteer serves as a liaison between the gaming community and the library; ensuring a library presence at these meetings shows a commitment that the library is an active partner in this program and allows your library to respond to your gaming community's needs more readily and in a much more organic fashion. Needless to say, this staff member/volunteer should either be a member of your library's gaming programming stakeholders group or report to someone on that committee, as they are an invaluable bellwether about what is working, what isn't working, and what the library can do differently to further enhance the local gaming community's participation and interest.

2. The staff member/volunteer serves as a liaison between the gaming community and other library patrons, ensuring that the library-sponsored event remains open and welcoming not just to the existing gaming community but to other interested patrons as well. Too often a library starts a gaming club with much fanfare and excitement only to find that it is the same people who come to the meeting. It is no secret that board gaming has traditionally attracted people who might be considered socially awkward or introverted. Also, an existing gaming group coming to the library, although helping kickstart your own program, will feature a cast of regulars who are already known to each other. As a result, there might be a conscious or unconscious bias against new members. Having a member of the library staff or volunteer visibly on hand to help welcome newcomers and integrate them into the group's activities can help overcome any of these real or perceived roadblocks to new members.

3. The staff member/volunteer serves as an ambassador for the idea that games and play belong at the library just as much as books, DVDs, and other media. In chapter 4 we introduced the term "dogfooding" as a process by which a company shows its faith in the product they are selling by using it themselves—for example, employees at a dog food company feeding its own dog food to their dogs. Here the concept serves a dual purpose: on the one hand, by having a regular library

staff or volunteer presence at these events, the library is signaling that games are important parts of the library's collection; at the same time, the library is actively defending the belief that play is not only acceptable in the workplace but something to be encouraged, even championed. Did that staff member just get paid to play games? Yes, they did. But does such activity align with the mission, vision, and goals of our institution? If you have successfully made your case with your boss, your administration, and your library stakeholders, absolutely it does (see chapter 2 for a longer discussion about this topic and strategies you can employ in making your case for gaming at the library).

⑥ Outfitting Your Gaming Club

Now that you've organized, scheduled, and promoted a regular gaming club meeting at your library, it's time to figure out how you will outfit it. For the various models of setting up a circulating library gaming materials collection, please consult chapter 4. While it is not uncommon for gaming club members to bring their own games to these meetings, as the host you should always plan on bringing a core group of games that people can play. You may also want to consider debuting new board game acquisitions at your regular gaming club meetings, as many of these titles are likely to be familiar to someone in the group and they will be able to help introduce the game and facilitate play with the other attendees.

As mentioned in chapter 4, your gaming club is an invaluable source for collection development, so it's important to incorporate their input and feedback into any acquisitions plan you may have for purchasing library gaming materials. At the Westport Library, we created a curated "Wish List" that our gaming group members could add suggestions to—more than half of our new games purchases would come from this community-generated list.

⑥ Beyond Gaming Club: "Learn to Play" Events and Other Forms of Outreach

Earlier in this chapter we discussed how board gaming groups can tend toward being somewhat insular if left to their own devices and that library staff should make every available effort to serve as intermediaries between your gaming collections and programs and your patrons. One of the best ways to accomplish this is by incorporating various outreach events into your library gaming programming. A simple form of outreach is to offer a "Learn to Play" event to the general public, where people who may be inexperienced with modern board games can learn how to play some of the more popular titles such as Catan, Ticket to Ride, Carcassonne, or Pandemic. The key to being able to support events like these is to make sure you have enough copies of each board game you are demonstrating in order to accommodate all of the people who might want to participate—again consult chapter 3 for strategies on acquiring library gaming materials from vendors and your friendly local game store, but you may also want to enlist your gaming group members to see if they can bring in personal copies of the game being featured for the event. At any rate, you should be prepared to have some circulating copies of any game being featured in this way, as it is very likely that once people have been introduced to it, they may want to keep playing it at home.

You will also want to have one facilitator on hand for each copy of the board game being used. These facilitators would ideally have played the game before and are therefore familiar with the rules themselves, or they could simply be good at picking up new games on the fly. Knowing how many copies of the game you can muster and how many facilitators you'll need as a result should give you a good sense of what your capacity for such an event should be, so you can then make sure you limit or cap registration if you require library patrons to sign up or preregister for your events. Remember that managing your patrons' expectations is an important consideration when planning "hands-on" library programming—this is true not just for gaming programming but any kind of event involving experiential learning. Although as a librarian there's nothing more exciting than sponsoring a program that garners a lot of interest, as an attendee there's nothing more frustrating than going to a gaming event and having to wait forever to get a chance to play.

If you are unable to control the amount of people coming to your event, consider having some familiar and easy-to-play backup games on hand for people who do have to wait. Games like Connect Four, Battleship, or Sorry can be acquired for very little money and are therefore good candidates for these kinds of "standby" games; if your library runs any video game programming, this is also an excellent opportunity to bring out one of your consoles and let people play or watch while they are waiting for their chance to play.

Themed Game Events and Local Tournaments

For more experienced board game players, you may want to consider offering "next level" events where they get a chance to play rare or unusual versions of certain games. For example, the popular railway-building board game Ticket to Ride comes in several different varieties, each of them allowing players to compete in different areas of the world: the United States, Europe, Asia, Africa, Germany, the Nordic Countries, India, Switzerland, the Netherlands, the United Kingdom, and Pennsylvania. Many gaming conferences offer some kind of "Around the World" type of event involving playing multiple versions of Ticket to Ride—it would be easy to adapt this into a library gaming event. The library could even print a passport for each player so that they could record their scores from each different area of the world they played, with prizes being awarded to anyone who successfully played through every map being featured that evening.

Catan (née Settlers of Catan) is another board game with multiple game boards, variants, and scenarios, which would make it an excellent candidate for this kind of event. Not only do you have the classic expansions to the game—Seafarers, Cities & Knights, Traders & Barbarians, and Explorers & Pirates—but there are also several historical versions featuring Ancient Rome, the American Old West, and the Stone Age. There is even a *Star Trek*–themed version of Catan! The cooperative disease-fighting game Pandemic also has multiple expansions—including On the Brink, In the Lab, and State of Emergency—and alternate versions including one set in nineteenth-century Iberia and an H. P. Lovecraft–themed version called Reign of Cthulhu.

"Legacy" Games and the Library: Like Oil and Water or PB and J?

Pandemic has a unique version of itself called Pandemic: Legacy. "Legacy" board games are a brand-new twist on the medium, as unlike regular board games where after each game the board and its components are reset, each legacy game changes permanently every time you play it. Each player decision makes irreversible changes to a legacy game, which can result in changes to the game board, destruction of various components (such as—gasp!—tearing up game cards), and even the introduction of new rules and objectives halfway through the game. If that weren't enough, legacy board games have an underlying story arc—patterned after the television season—which is only fully explored after the players have played the board game a certain amount of times, at which point the story is concluded and the game is "over."

The first legacy-style board game was created in 2011, when Hasbro asked Rob Daviau, one of its game designers, to come up with a new edition of the classic board game Risk. The result was Risk: Legacy, which shocked the board game world by asking players to tear up cards, throw away components, and write on the game board with a permanent marker; it also delighted the same players with new rules and components, which were revealed over the course of fifteen sessions of play. The concept was such a hit with board gamers that Daviau was asked by the creator of Pandemic (Matthew Leacock) to design a legacy version for his already-popular board game, which involves a team of specialists working together to try and rid the world of four diseases in the middle of a worldwide outbreak.

Like Risk: Legacy, Pandemic: Legacy is meant to be played by the same group of players over and over again; unlike Risk: Legacy, however, Pandemic: Legacy follows a year-long storyline that the specialists play through month by month. As Pandemic is a cooperative board game, players either win or lose together as a team. Therefore if the team wins in the January episode, they move on to February. If the team loses any given month, however, they must replay the month's scenario (although if they lose again, they automatically advance to the next month). Depending on how the players fare, the game either becomes easier or more difficult as they go—for example, there is a special aid package that is only unlocked if the players hit a losing streak of four or more games—but again like in Risk: Legacy, the effects of each game are permanent and carry through until the next time the game is played. It would be a shame to spoil the overall plot of Pandemic: Legacy, but let's just say that there are several major developments during play, each of which significantly changes how the game is played and ratchets up the emotional intensity as well.

Legacy board games are not just a new kind of board game but a new form of narrative as well, one which presents an interesting conundrum for librarians. How do you collect a board game that is playable only for so many times, and how would a library justify purchasing a game (Pandemic: Legacy retails for around $50) that at the very most only four patrons could play? Just the thought of circulating a copy of this game would give preservation and conservation librarians nightmares as the players duly ripped up or destroyed components as the game instructions told them to!

Unfortunately this is a conundrum that is probably not going away, however, as the success of Risk: Legacy and especially that of Pandemic: Legacy have spawned a new generation of legacy-style board games: Gloomhaven, a Dungeons & Dragons-like adventuring game; Android: Netrunner—Terminal Directive, a cyberpunk murder mystery for two players; and Seafall, a competitive high seas exploration game from Rob Daviau. There are even more legacy board games currently under development—such as Charterstone, a village-building legacy game by Jamey Stegmaier, and Centauri Saga: Abandoned, a cooperative space exploration board game by Constantine Kevorque. Meanwhile, the hotly anticipated Pandemic: Legacy Season Two arrived in stores in the summer of 2017. While it remains to be seen whether legacy-style board games will become a permanent genre of the medium, they are an important subcategory of board gaming in the meantime, so libraries that collect and circulate board games will have to think creatively to accommodate these kinds of games.

⑥ Binge-Play with Us: Legacy Games as Library Event

One potential solution to the problems posed by legacy board games is not to circulate them at all but to play through them as part of a library-sponsored event. For example, the library would announce that it will be starting a round of Pandemic: Legacy and signing up a roster of players for the twelve-plus sessions needed to complete the overall narrative. Although the game only allows a maximum of four players, because players might not be available for every session, it might be prudent to sign up a couple of designated alternates as well; each session would include a library staff member or volunteer familiar with the game who would serve as facilitator and help keep track of various rule changes as the story progresses. If there was sufficient interest, the library could sponsor multiple parallel campaigns—however, the library would need to acquire an additional copy of the game for each group playing its way through. In this sense each group would be its own little library gaming program, similar to sponsoring a regular role-playing group (see chapter 9 for more information on RPGs in the library). Since the game itself is technically a nonreturnable item, the library could either choose to foot the expense as part of its library gaming or programming budget or it could ask each group to split the cost of the board game as a participation fee.

⑥ Sponsoring Local Gaming Tournaments @ Your Library

Another board game event that would appeal to an established community of gamers would be a local gaming tournament. The library would pick one of the more popular competitive board games—such as Catan, Dominion, 7 Wonders, Race for the Galaxy, or Ticket to Ride—and set up a day-long or multi-day tournament where participants play this game several times. Alternatively, players could all play several rounds, with each round featuring a different board game. There is an even more challenging board game tournament format, made popular by the Great Canadian Board Game Blitz (www .gcbgb.ca), a five-game format in which one player chooses the game for each round from a list of five to six unique board games, but for the sake of this chapter, we will try to keep things as simple as possible.

There are many different ways of organizing tournament play, but the most common tournament format is some combination of group play with a knockout or playoff bracket. For group play, try to make it so that each person is able to play at least three games—not only does this average out the baleful effects of bad luck in any one game, but it also ensures that everyone who participates in the tournament gets to spend the majority of their time playing and not simply spectating as they wait for their turn. Just like in the case of a "Learn to Play" event, this means you need to estimate how many copies of the game you'll need so that group play can all happen simultaneously—please refer back to this earlier section for strategies on obtaining additional games for this kind of event.

Unlike "Learn to Play" events, however, you will not need one staff member or volunteer for each game, as tournament play is predicated on some basic understanding of how the game is being played. Be sure to have some staff roving during group play to answer any questions or rules clarifications as the games are being played, however, and resolve any conflicts that may arise—friendly or otherwise.

⊚ Winning Is the Easy Part:
How to Keep Score for Tournament Rankings

Again, there are many different ways to score tournament play for the purpose of ranking, but for the sake of time, space, and sanity, we will only suggest two of them here. Perhaps the simplest system of ranking is to assign a point value for each place achieved at the end of the game—for example, five points for first place, three points for second place, one point for third place, and zero points for fourth place—and to add these values up at the end of group play. Since most board games have running point totals for each player during gameplay, an alternate method of tallying is to add these totals up instead and rank players accordingly. The advantage of the former method is that it prioritizes winning over anything else, whereas the latter method measures the relative quality of each win when compared to other players. The disadvantage of using the latter method is that a player with fewer wins could actually end up ranking ahead of a player who won more or even all of their games in group play. How you choose to organize your tournament and score your rankings is entirely up to you, but be sure to make these rules and regulations transparent and available to all of your participants so that no one is able to cry foul about this aspect of the event.

After group play, you can either declare the player with the highest total as the winner of the tournament or select a certain number of the highest-ranking players to move on to a knockout stage or playoff round. For most multiplayer board games, a playoff round is usually the optimal format, since again it allows as many people to play at the same time as possible and minimize people waiting to play. How many players you want to admit to this second round of play is entirely up to you and your fellow tournament organizers, but to make the tournament competitive, you probably want to limit it to no more than the amount of players it would take to fill out four games—this will result in four winners, who could then play-off against each other in a final round if desired. Again, this format can be expanded, contracted, or otherwise tweaked to your heart's content, and readers are encouraged to look at a universe of examples available not just for competitive board game play but any other kind of competition for inspiration. The example that we have walked through here—i.e., a round of group play, a knockout round, and a final round—is suitable for either a long all-day tournament (eight hours) or a more comfortable two-day tournament (four hours each day), so you can use it as the basis for your own tournament planning purposes.

⊚ To the Victors: Prizes for Your Library Gaming Tournament

How you wish to reward your tournament winners depends entirely on your budget for this event. Is this a library-funded event, or will you ask each participant for an entrance fee? Even a nominal fee could help offset the costs of acquiring extra copies of the game, for instance, or go toward the procurement of tournament rewards. One common prize for a board game tournament is a deluxe or collector's edition of the game being played or a gift certificate to your community's friendly local game store. While these are great prizes, you may also want to incorporate the library somehow into your prize structure—say, for example, the patron's choice from the library's selection of advance reader's copies (or ARCs) or some dedicated time using the library's 3-D printers or virtual reality facilities. If your library does have a MakerSpace, perhaps they could create a custom game board or special game pieces to commemorate the tournament that could be awarded as prizes or even awards of participation for everyone who does sign up and play. There are many custom board game files on 3-D printing template websites such as Thingiverse, so that would be a good place to start for inspiration. The possibilities are endless, but try to think of a prize structure that can let everyone walk out the door with something, even if it's just a badge or a token.

◎ Other Special Gaming Events @ Your Library—Enter Wil Wheaton

If the board gaming world had a sacred calendar, it would have two major holidays: International Tabletop Day in April and International Games Week in November. International Tabletop Day was started in 2013 by game designer Boyan Radakovich, one of the producers of TableTop, an enormously popular web series about board games hosted by Wil Wheaton (yes, that Wil Wheaton, of *Star Trek: The Next Generation* and *The Big Bang Theory* fame) and published on Felicia Day's YouTube channel Geek & Sundry. As the host of the *TableTop* show, Wil Wheaton invites a group of celebrity guests to sit down and play a board game with him. Over the past four seasons, Wheaton has managed to introduce followers of the show to almost eighty new board games—not only has this benefited gamers, who can use *TableTop* as a way of seeing whether they would like a certain game by watching other people play it first, but it has also been a boon to retailers, as there is a boost in sales for each game after being featured on the show. Indeed, after the strategy game Tsuro was demonstrated in season 1, the publisher literally sold out of its stock reserves and the game was briefly unavailable for sale in Europe as they scrambled to produce more copies.

As an aside, it would be interesting to see if libraries that circulate board games have seen any increased circulation or demands for purchase for the games featured on this show as well. As of the writing of this book, no one has tried to correlate these data yet, perhaps because the data set of available lending libraries with gaming collections is still too small. Nevertheless, this makes *TableTop* a potentially useful source for collection development purposes, both as a curated list of new games that may be of interest to your library community (see chapter 3 for more about the library gaming collection development process and other such resources for discovering and reviewing new games) as well as a "gamers' advisory" kind of curated resource you can recommend to your patrons. One word of caution, however: although mostly innocuous, the banter on *TableTop* can unexpectedly veer into adult territory, with a generous amount of swearing and the occasional bit of sexual innuendo, so you may want to warn your patrons before watching the show on YouTube with the whole family!

As Wheaton observes: "So I keep hearing about this thing called the 'TableTop' effect, and I think that we're helping. And I'm not saying it's because of me. It's because we're making it possible for people to see how much fun it is to play these games, so people are starting game groups. People who were gamers and maybe stopped gaming are starting to game again, and it's sort of taking on a little bit of a life of its own" (Clark

2013). International Tabletop Day was envisioned as a way to give people the opportunity to find this sense of community by organizing open board game play across as many friendly venues as possible—mostly vendors and friendly local game stores, but as the event has gained momentum over the years, other institutions have gotten involved as well, including libraries. Geek & Sundry celebrates each International Tabletop Day with twenty-four hours of gaming that is streamed live on their channel, so at the very least your library may want to link to this stream or designate a venue in your library space where people can watch it. They also feature a list of games that will be played during the twenty-four-hour livestream, so you can try to get these titles in advance if you're interested in playing along. For example, International Tabletop Day 2017 played through the following games: Fuse, King of Tokyo, Rhino Hero, Dread Draw, Codenames, Dread RPG, Tsuro, Attack on Titan, and Dark Souls, with an eighteen-hour session of the strategy board game Twilight Imperium.

Libraries interested in setting up International Tabletop Day events should consult the official ITTD website: www.tabletopday.com, where they can register their location as a community participant and download event logos and other promotional materials from the media folder. Geek & Sundry works with retailers to offer exclusive gaming items for the event, such as special expansions to existing popular board games, new or limited edition microgames made specially for ITTD, and custom or collectible gaming components—although libraries are not eligible to obtain these, if your friendly local game shop is partnering with Geek & Sundry for the event, you may want to reach out and see whether they would be willing to co-host the event. Not only could this help raise visibility in cross-promoting the library at the game store and vice versa, but it also brings more gaming expertise to assist with hosting such an event (please refer back to chapter 5 for more information on community partnerships, particularly with friendly local game shops or FLGS's).

◎ Don't Forget the Librarians!

Not to be outdone by the likes of Wesley Crusher, librarians have their own gaming holiday at the other end of the calendar. International Games Day (IGD) was established by the Games and Gaming Round Table of the American Library Association in 2012, an expansion of National Games Day, which was started by librarians Jenny Levine and Scott Nicholson in 2007 originally as an attempt to set a world's record for the largest number of people playing the same game at the same time. Since 2012 IGD has grown to involve not just the ALA but the Australian Library and Information Association, Nordic Game Week, and L'Associazione Italiana Biblioteche, as well as individual libraries participating from fifty-three countries, sponsoring events on all seven continents—the event has also expanded to include programming not just on one day but encompassing several days or, in some cases, an entire week of special library games programming. In recognition of this growth, International Games Day became International Games Week (IGW) starting in 2017, recognizing an entire week of activities from October 29 to November 4.

Although International Games Week is not exclusively a board gaming event, sponsors donate thousands of copies of board games every year so that libraries who are not able to acquire gaming materials on their own are able to participate in IGW. Libraries can sign up to register their location as officially participating in the event at games.ala.org/register-for-igw, with links to their own programming during International Games Week; libraries in need of board game donations can also indicate whether they are interested in receiving copies of featured games for that year's event. There are also myriad promotional materials and branding available for librarians to download and use to promote their own IGW events. High-profile events such as International Games Week are an excellent way to highlight all of your library's gaming activities, so by no means restrict yourself to just board gaming when planning your participation but include collectible card games, video games, role-playing games, and other gaming activities as you see fit. If you need additional inspiration, check out the list of libraries participating in IGW and see what kind of programming they are offering. Remember that one of the most wonderful things about libraries is that we are all always able to benefit from each other's successes and learn from one another's mistakes, so by all means let other institutions that have already taken the gaming plunge help inform your own implementation.

Board Game Events and Thematic Programming

Thus far we have discussed library gaming programming for specific gaming events at your library, be it a local or community club or in tandem with a larger national or international event. Another strategy for introducing board gaming to your community is to incorporate it into other library programming when thematically appropriate. For example, if your library is doing any children's, teen, or MakerSpace programming about *Star Wars*—say, to commemorate the release of a new *Star Wars* film, to recognize *Star Wars* Read Day in October, or to celebrate the Fourth of May (aka *Star Wars* Day, which turned the ultimate groaner of a pun into an unofficial holiday for the franchise, i.e., "May the Fourth Be With You")—you may want to consider adding some *Star Wars*–themed board gaming to your programming offerings. Fortunately for you, your choices are not constrained to just *Star Wars* Monopoly or Trivial Pursuit, as several quality *Star Wars* gaming products have arrived on the market in recent years. Perhaps the most famous of these is the enormously popular X-Wing Miniatures game. *Star Wars*: X-Wing is a miniature war game designed by Jay Little that made its debut at GenCon in 2012. Players command various spaceships from the *Star Wars* universe in a quick but exciting three-dimensional dogfight. Part board game, part collectible miniature set, X-Wing comes with various game expansions featuring various ships from the *Star Wars* franchise—including unique ships such as Han Solo's *Millennium Falcon* and bounty hunter Boba Fett's *Slave One*.

Not only is X-Wing easy to learn and fun to play, but it also tends to draw a crowd of onlookers curious to see what's going on with all of the spaceships. Although the stock board game and its supplements come with two-dimensional maps and a selection of three-dimensional cardboard obstacles (such as asteroids) that can be used for gameplay, one of the respects in which the X-Wing game shines is the sheer amount of creativity it allows in designing backdrops or environments for the board game. In fact, there is an entire Maker movement dedicated to the art of making custom "niches" for the *Star Wars*: X-Wing game, making the game an interesting choice not only for its recognizable theme and ease of play but also because it allows you to engage both the players and the Makers in your community at the same time. This is a topic that merits further exploration, and to be sure we will dedicate an entire chapter to how to incorporate your library's

MakerSpace into your library gaming programming and vice versa, but in the meantime let's remember to be mindful of exactly these kinds of synergies in our library's activities and programming.

War (Gaming): What Is It Good For?

By extension any other kind of miniature wargaming is similarly full of this kind of gaming/Making potential, although by losing the *Star Wars* brand, you may have to work a little harder on selling the activities to a broader audience than those who would self-select for such an event, such as history buffs or war gaming enthusiasts. War gaming occupies an interesting continuum along the board gaming spectrum, as there are war games that come as complete playable packages right out of the box—for example, Hasbro's venerable and still-popular World War II board game Axis & Allies or the Cold War détente thriller Twilight Struggle—while there are other kinds of war games that require a significant Maker or crafting component to assemble and paint all of the materials necessary to play. To be sure, this latter kind of war gaming is as much its own hobby as it is gaming per se, but because there is such great potential overlap between war gaming crafting activities and your library MakerSpace, we would be remiss in not recommending this genre of gaming as a way to engage your community—especially in terms of what different demographics you may be able to reach as a result. For if *Star Wars* gaming would guarantee kids under a certain age, war games programming could be of specific interest to older generations, not only for the historical context but also the "old-school" terrain crafting, which is functionally similar to model railroading. We will cover these and other various subheadings of Making activities that can actively support your library gaming programming in chapter 11.

Surely war games aren't necessarily a topic for all audiences, however. So when would war gaming be appropriate for a library community? A great example would be if your community played a historically significant role in a battle or military action—this can be relatively easy for communities on the East Coast, given their relative age compared to towns and cities in the Midwest and on the Pacific Coast. For example, if your community is commemorating an event from the Revolutionary or Civil War, you may want to incorporate some war gaming programming at your library by painting miniatures and assembling a battlefield diorama that can illustrate the specific battle or event of historic interest. You may want to exercise some discretion when offering war gaming featuring wars for which there are still active veterans, in deference to soldiers who may have suffered from post-traumatic stress disorder.

A fascinating example of taking the library war gaming programming to the next level and making it a truly immersive experience is literally happening as this chapter is being written: on June 24, 2017, at the Andrew Carnegie Free Library & Music Hall, library patrons of all ages came together for a program called "Defend Library Hill"—a live historical reenactment Civil War Trust Generations Event:

> Calling all recruits to preserve the Union! With Robert E. Lee's army pushing through Central Pennsylvania, the time to serve your country is now. Enlist in the Union Army for a day, and experience what it was like to be a Civil War soldier. Recruits will enlist, learn the school of the soldier, experience camp life, visit the regimental doctor, and earn you honorable discharge from the army.

Share your passion for history with your child, niece, grandson or friends for this special "Generations" event, sponsored by the Civil War Trust and the Andrew Carnegie Free Library & Music Hall. Some lucky kids will even get to don a uniform! As always, our "Cadet Conference" format employs hands-on activities and stresses teamwork, leadership, ethics and responsibility lessons.

Join us as we bring the Civil War and the Thomas Espy Grand Army of the Republic Post to life. (Bruce 2017)

◎ Other Thematic Gaming Programming @ Your Library

Of course not every gaming event at your library needs to tie into history or the latest Hollywood blockbuster. Look for other kinds of thematic adjacencies in your library programming and see if offering a board gaming activity would either add to or detract from the event in question that's being offered. We have already discussed how to evaluate and assess your gaming programming, so be mindful of the time, effort, and space required to incorporate board gaming into existing library programming. Even though in this day and age you can almost always find a board game that can tie in thematically to your library programming, the last thing you want to do is distract your patrons from the main event. That being said, if the program in question involves any kind of waiting or separate stations of activity, board gaming might be a welcome addition—especially if you choose board games that are relatively quick to learn and play, so that patrons who are coming to enjoy the primary program don't feel they have to choose between playing a game and missing out on their desired library activity.

For example, is there a short and sweet board game that can be played as library patrons wait for an event to begin? A common activity among hard-core gamers when they go to conferences like PAX or GenCon is to bring a selection of "lightweight" games with them so that they can occupy their time while sitting down in line and waiting for the next big event to take place. If your library can build a repertoire of such light board or card games, these might be easy to deploy in such cases to assist with crowd management. While by no means necessary, how much more fun would it be if the theme of these games could somehow relate to the programming at hand!

◎ Conclusion: You Will Never Be Bored with Board Games

After this whirlwind tour of board games in the library, I hope you see that the board gaming hobby has come a long way since the last time you may have played a game. This is almost certainly true for your patrons as well. How, then, to introduce twenty years of evolution and revolution to your library community? For starters, be sure to leverage your existing gaming community or friendly local game store, but also do not be afraid to take the time and effort to familiarize your staff with these new kinds of games as well, keeping in mind that they will serve as the points of interaction between patrons and your library gaming collections. Also, try to incorporate gaming organically into the overall library programming planning process—look for opportunities for synergy with other departments' programming, particularly with your library's MakerSpace, but don't be afraid to carve a separate space out for gaming in the library as well. A robust and growing library gaming program will be both complementary and supplementary in nature as well as stand on its own.

⑥ Key Points

- You can kick-start your board gaming programming by enlisting the help/partnership of a local board gaming club.
- Whether or not your staff is responsible for running your library's board gaming club, be sure to schedule a regular staff presence at these events as instructors, facilitators, and participants.
- "Learn to Play" events, where one or a small group of thematically related board games are introduced, can help introduce your community to new kinds of board games.
- Legacy games, the newest form of board gaming, combines the fun of traditional gaming with the thrills of a movie or television show, with the results of one game carrying through into the next to form a campaign narrative arc.
- Tournaments attract participants from the entire region and beyond and can be very competitive.
- Consider participating in worldwide gaming events like International Tabletop Day or International Games Week to receive assistance with publicity (and free gaming materials!).

⑥ References

American Library Association Games and Gaming Round Table. 2018. "IGW History." *Games in Libraries* (blog). games.ala.org/igw-history/ (accessed January 2, 2018).

Bruce, Andrew. 2017. "Civil War Generations: Defend Library Hill." *10mm Wargaming* (blog), June 12. www.civilwar.org/events/generations-pittsburgh.

Clark, Noelene. 2013. "International TableTop Day: Wil Wheaton Wants You to Play Board Games." *LA Times*, March 7. herocomplex.latimes.com/games/international-tabletop-day -wil-wheaton-wants-you-to-play-board-games/.

CHAPTER 7

How to Implement Video Game Programming in Your Library

IN THIS CHAPTER

▷ Insert Several Hundred Quarters to Continue

▷ This Is Our Idea of Fun: Playing Video Games

▷ PlayStation FTW?

▷ In Defense of the Xbox

▷ Don't Forget the Switch!

▷ Which Console Is Best for the Library?

▷ Don't Forget the Wii/Wii U

▷ Other Retro Platforms and Emulators

▷ Computer Gaming in the Library

▷ Give Me Steam—A Public Library Quandary?

▷ LAN Partying Like It's 1999

▷ Beyond the Shmups: Choosing Your Games

▷ Minecraft Is Its Own Beast

▷ Roblox—Minecraft Meets LEGO Meets . . . Second Life?

I N 2013 JUSTIN HOENKE ACQUIRED a Ms. Pac-Man arcade machine for the Chattanooga Public Library in Chattanooga, Tennessee, where he was teen librarian at the time. Although Justin had already met with great success in developing library video game programming with console and computer games, nevertheless he felt that something was missing:

> Setting up home video game console in a library sort of replicates the video game arcade experience. You've got the gaming experience, the community setting, and the excitement. But there's just something about standing around those old wooden cabinets that's lost with console gaming. There's a connection and a community built around those machines that can't be replicated with other forms of gaming. That's why last month I obtained an original 1981 Ms. Pac-Man arcade machine for the 2nd Floor of my library. (Hoenke 2013a)

This unorthodox addition to the Chattanooga Public Library's second floor proved to be a breakaway hit, generating plaudits not just from the library community but from one of the original co-creators of the Ms. Pac-Man arcade game himself: "I just found out about your Ms. Pac-Man at your library," Steve Golson wrote in an e-mail to Justin Hoenke, which he screencapped and Tweeted. "Outstanding idea! I was one of the designers of Ms. Pac-Man. Wow, that was a loooong time ago. Keep up the great work with the teens." Teens immediately flocked to the new machine, trying their best to one-up each other's high scores. Justin saw something else going on at the same time: "To see an original Ms. Pac-Man up and running in a library is like looking into a time machine. You see how it was built, how the game operates, and if you're lucky enough to have a librarian around, see how the electronics and circuits and wires all fit together in order to make the game work. You get to peer into just how far technology has come over the past 40 years" (Hoenke 2013b).

While having the Ms. Pac-Man game itself as part of the library's collection was no doubt fun, the physical presence of the arcade game in the library as a social and technological artifact brought a whole new dimension to a gaming experience that could

My wife and my son defend the planet from Space Invaders at the American Classic Arcade Museum in Laconia, New Hampshire.

be otherwise replicated nowadays in a web browser or a smartphone: the dimension of experiential learning. Indeed, inspired by Justin's example, when I was in charge of the Westport Library MakerSpace, we acquired a broken pinball machine on Craigslist—for the low, low price of $50 no less!—with the express purpose of learning how it worked well enough in order to fix it up and restore it back to a playable condition (we will discuss this project and similar possibilities for involving your library MakerSpace in gaming activities in chapter 11).

As you can see, bringing video games to the library can be as simple as adding a gaming console and a few games to your collections. However, video games can bring with them a sense of extended community and a hands-on experiential learning component that we are only just beginning to appreciate fully in library circles. It is with this holistic mental model of video gaming in mind that we will approach this chapter. First we will look at the current state of console gaming, recommending particular platforms that are especially library-friendly and trying to intuit what the gaming market might look like in three to five years. Then we will look at the various special cases of video games: retro console games, computer games (i.e., for PC or Mac), and virtual worlds such as Minecraft or Roblox. Following this chapter will be a chapter-long case study taking a closer look at the red-hot phenomenon of "augmented reality" games such as Pokémon GO (chapter 8) and how you can design your library's gaming programs and outreach activities so as to maximum your community's return when playing these kinds of games in or around the library.

What we can't do in the space of this chapter, however, is provide any magical formulae or "one size fits all" solutions for implementing video gaming programming at your library. Not only are video games, consoles, and accessories expensive, but other aspects necessary to support video gaming at the library—such as ample power, reliable wired and wireless Internet, and simply good IT support for set-up, troubleshooting, and maintenance—are often beyond any one librarian's control. Instead, what we focus on providing you here is the best possible toolkit for whatever your library can finance and support.

This Is Our Idea of Fun: Playing Video Games

Now let us take a brief overview of the current state of video gaming, as well as a look at potential future trends in the hobby. According to the 2017 report *Essential Facts About the Computer and Video Game Industry* published by the Entertainment Software Association:

- Sixty-five percent of American households are home to someone who plays video games regularly, and 67 percent of American households own a device used to play video games.
- Gamers age eighteen or older represent 72 percent of the video game-playing population, and the average gamer is thirty-five years old.
- Adult women represent a greater portion of the video game-playing population (31 percent) than boys under age eighteen (18 percent).
- Sixty-seven percent of parents play video games with their children at least once a week.
- Seventy-one percent of parents feel video games positively impact their child's life.

- The majority of parents (85 percent) are very familiar with the Entertainment Software Rating Board video game rating system, and among them, 96 percent are very confident the rating system is accurate.
- Fifty-three percent of the most frequent video game players report playing video games with others.
- Eleven percent of U.S. households own a virtual reality (VR) headset, and one-third of the most frequent video game players say they will buy a VR headset in the next year.
- Seventy-four percent of PC/console VR headset owners use their device to play single player video games.

These are extraordinary findings, especially considering the myriad stereotypes associated with gaming culture and the gamer demographic, as the data appear to refute many of them: for example, the notion that women are not interested in gaming or that gaming is inherently antisocial. Clearly we are in the midst of a cultural shift whereby gaming culture is becoming a mainstream phenomenon and not the exclusive domain of any one demographic. On the contrary, gaming is becoming increasingly multi-generational, gender-balanced, and social, and therefore our library gaming programming should not just reflect these trends but embrace and build upon them.

Another interesting statistic from the ESA report is that only 48 percent of American households have a dedicated game console (Entertainment Software Association 2017). Considering that the console gaming market is currently fragmented between three major platforms—i.e., Sony's PlayStation 4 (or PS4), Microsoft's Xbox One, and Nintendo's Switch—this flies in the face of the common objection to the idea of libraries acquiring and lending gaming consoles that "everybody already owns one" and represents a timely window of opportunity for public libraries to fill a void. Indeed, one of the major reasons even gamer-friendly households shy away from making a new console purchase isn't just the initial expenditure on hardware and accessories, which isn't insubstantial, but a complicated sort of fear of missing out (FOMO) peculiar to gaming culture where there is a reluctance to back the "losing" platform. This fear is often accentuated by the fact that some popular video game franchises are either platform-specific or are released on other platforms weeks or months after the initial release, which means that gamers miss the collective sense of virtual community that surrounds the launch of a new video game.

ⓢ PlayStation FTW?

So which console is the best bet for a library to invest in? Well, it depends. If we are simply to purchase the most popular platform currently available, then the PlayStation 4 is the hands-down winner, capturing 51 percent of the console sales market in 2016, compared to the Xbox One's 26 percent share and Nintendo's 8 percent (Harding-Rolls 2017). Numbers can be deceiving, however, for the Nintendo Switch did not launch until spring of 2017 and has proven to be a runaway best-seller, suggesting that trends in console sales may be significantly different in 2017 and especially 2018. Sony has also worked closely with many independent game developers to bring exclusive content to the PS4 platform, which brings us back to the FOMO factor.

Another point in favor of acquiring a PlayStation 4 is the fact that it is the only console currently capable of supporting virtual reality. PlayStation VR has only been around for a year, but it has more than one hundred titles (or "experiences") already available in the PlayStation Store, with many more on the way. We will discuss virtual reality in greater detail later in this chapter, but suffice it to say that currently PlayStation VR is the easiest "out of the box" solution for virtual reality, with a second-generation headset already on sale in Japan.

In Defense of the Xbox

Although the PS4 is currently dominating the console market, the Xbox One X (as opposed to the Xbox One S, which is the "original" Xbox One) is actually the most powerful platform available. Xbox One is cross-compatible with Windows 10, which means many titles can be played across platforms with PC gamers. The Xbox's video processing power also makes it a great choice for video-streaming, an increasingly popular social activity that your library may or may not want to get more involved with as gaming social sharing websites such as Twitch compete with other forms of media for the next generation's attention and belie a multi-billion dollar market of online games consumption, including the burgeoning e-sports movement. The Xbox One is also backward compatible with a huge catalog of classic Xbox and Xbox 360 games, making it a double investment in a current console and retro gaming platform.

Don't Forget the Switch!

As mentioned above, the Nintendo Switch is still a relative newcomer to the console wars, having succeeded the commercially successful Wii console and the markedly less popular Wii U. What the Wii U promised and failed to do, however—that is, offer a console that could also double as a handheld game platform—the Nintendo Switch pulls off almost flawlessly, and like many Nintendo platforms is a great console for multiplayer gaming, with classics such as Mario Kart 8 and new offerings like Arms, which is a wildly imaginative take on the virtual boxing genre. Whereas third-party developers avoided the Wii and Wii U like the plague, Nintendo seems to have lured a critical mass of game developers into the fold this time around, which helps mightily when combatting gamers' FOMO. Nintendo Switch players can now enjoy playing popular titles such as Skyrim, L.A. Noire, Resident Evil Revelations, and NBA 2K18.

Which Console Is Best for the Library?

Clearly each of these three consoles has its own set of advantages and disadvantages, and in a perfect world a lending library would have at least one of each platform for its community to borrow and experiment with. But if you only had the funding to choose one, which should it be? In this case I would recommend the PlayStation 4, mostly because of its 3-D capabilities and its huge original catalog of games. If I had the budget for only two consoles, however, I would go with a PS4 and a Nintendo Switch, mostly because of the Switch's relative novelty (until recently it was selling out of most retail outlets on a fairly regular basis) and the ease of play for most of the titles under its umbrella.

⦿ Don't Forget the Wii/Wii U

That being said, just because the Wii and Wii U never enjoyed the breakaway commercial success that Nintendo had always hoped for doesn't mean they aren't fairly intuitive platforms with titles that are easy to play and appeal to a broad range of both experienced and casual gamers. They're also still to be found in abundance in retro game shops and online, where obsolete console game systems and their titles enjoy a brisk secondary market. Both the Wii and Wii U have many multiplayer games that are ideal for a library gaming event, such as Super Smash Bros. or Mario Kart—Smash can support up to eight players battling at once on the Wii U, and Mario Kart can support up to either two players on the Wii or up to four simultaneously local racers on the Wii U. Since the consoles are fairly easy to set up as well, they make for excellent choices to circulate out of the library.

⦿ Other Retro Platforms and Emulators

There are of course other older consoles to choose from when supporting retro gaming activities at your library—from the N64 to Sega Genesis to the Atari 2600, the veritable godfather of home gaming consoles. If you don't have the good fortune of knowing someone in your library community who can bring in one of these consoles to support your event, the good news is that many of them are now available for sale again as gaming companies realize that there is a great deal of money to be made in the retro game nostalgia market. The best thing about many of these "flashback" consoles is that they also come with a large assortment of games for that platform—for example, the Atari AR 3220 Flashback 8 Classic Game Console, which retails for $39.99, comes with a selection of 105 original Atari 2600 titles, including games made by Atari for the platform as well as third-party games designed by Activision and other companies.

Prior to the re-release of the original hardware, however, retro gamers usually had one of two options when they wanted to play an old game they didn't have the console for: backward compatibility on a current-generation console (such as the Xbox One and various original Xbox and Xbox 360 titles) or running an emulator on a computer. One can find software to emulate virtually any gaming console that was ever sold, along with the games to run on it via software. The problem with these emulators was that they were usually written by experts for a specific computer make/model and operating system, such that someone who wrote an Atari 2600 emulator for a Windows 95 PC back in the 1990s may not have thought to update the program and make sure it continued to run on a modern desktop machine. So at the very least, emulators require a bit of elbow grease to get working and in many cases actual computer skills to get them to run in a way that replicates the original gaming experience.

Given the intellectual property limbo that "out of print" materials fall into, the legality of creating and distributing such emulators has always been problematic, although a strong case could be made for being allowed to emulate software that is both no longer for sale and only able to run on an obsolete platform. Whatever their official copyright status, emulators can be incorporated into many MakerSpace gaming activities, including building your own retro arcade, which we will cover in chapter 11.

ⓖ Computer Gaming in the Library

Emulators of course aren't the only kind of computer gaming. Twenty-three percent of all video games sold in 2017 were for the PC (while we don't have reliable numbers for Mac game sales, alas, Apple desktop game sales are only a fraction of that of the PC market, as game developers by and large think of the Mac OS as an afterthought, although Apple more than makes up for this in the mobile gaming market). While computer games are usually difficult if not impossible to circulate due to installation requirements and anti-piracy keys that may only be associated with one or a limited number of machines, the library may still support computer gaming in the library in a number of ways, including allowing patrons to access their own Steam gaming accounts on library workstations, hosting LAN parties for multiplayer PC games, and facilitating 3-D or virtual reality gaming at the library, a topic we will cover in greater depth in chapter 11.

ⓖ Give Me Steam—A Public Library Quandary?

Do you Steam? Started in 2003 by the Valve Corporation (creators of the immensely popular video games Portal and Half-Life) as a platform to facilitate pushing out updates to its online games such as Counter-Strike, Steam quickly became the premier digital distribution platform for computer gaming, accounting for more than 75 percent of all PC game sales and downloads, with 150 million registered accounts and 17.5 million concurrent users as of late 2017. Gamers are able to discover and purchase new games—as well as older games and classic titles, which are often heavily discounted on a regularly recurring basis or offered for free as part of a larger promotional cycle for that gaming franchise or developer—through the Steam Store, which licenses the game content to the player's Steam account and allows them to download and play the game on any compatible device.

This is, of course, where the library gets involved. Allowing patrons to access their own Steam accounts on public PC workstations depends very much on how locked down your public computers are in the library, but often there are some machines in the building that allow enough patron access in order to permit this activity; for example, the MakerSpace, where patrons may need greater freedom in running programs they need for coding, design, or other experiential learning activities, may have less restricted machines that would permit patrons to log in using their own Steam accounts. Of course, when public libraries talk about being more STEAM-friendly, this isn't exactly what they're talking about! The dangers of allowing patrons to download their own content to library workstations are well-known enough, but insofar as gamers may have libraries of mature and/or explicit-rated gaming material in their personal Steam libraries this may place library staff in the awkward position of having to police gaming content on their public machines.

Nevertheless Steam does offer an interesting possibility whereby the library could create its own account and curate a selection of library-friendly games that could then be made available on select public workstations, as Steam does permit library sharing among several machines using the same log-in credentials. The only caveat is that in such a scenario each game could only have one user playing it at any given time, similar to a library ebook only being available to one library patron at a time. This would allow libraries to "offer" gaming materials for PC gamers to try out in the comfort of their own public library before deciding whether to buy the games for themselves.

⊚ LAN Partying Like It's 1999

The Local Area Network or LAN party has a long and venerable history, tracing back to single-player Unix games that kept scoreboards on a central server. The Atari ST game MIDI Maze, however, offered the first example of a multiplayer networked game, spawning an entire genre of "deathmatch" first-person shooter games, such as id Software's Doom, that blended stand-alone one-player games with an ongoing story with multiplayer shoot-'em-up arenas where players could actually cooperate to solve the game's narrative objectives together. While Macintosh computers were very easily networked and actually were an important part of the early LAN party gaming scene, it was with the advent of Windows 95 and low-cost ethernet cards that the phenomenon truly took off and gained a life of its own in the mid- to late 1990s.

As LAN parties tend to require a lot of space and power, as well as ample ethernet connections, the library is an ideal place to host such an event, although you may want to consider doing so after the library closes and making it an all-night "lock-in" event if you don't have a large enough room that is soundproofed enough to minimize disruption to other library patrons. There are many detailed resources on the Internet that can help you set up a LAN (such as the following wikiHow article: www.wikihow.com/Host-a-LAN-Party), but at its most basic you will need at least:

1. two or more computers with network cards;
2. network cables;
3. an ethernet hub, switch, or router; and
4. adequate power.

If you're in luck, someone on your library IT staff will be a LAN party veteran if you're not, or one of your gamer attendees will be. There's nothing like leveraging the technical expertise of your teenaged gamer demographic, and it's events just like these that can help draw them out of the woodwork and into the library!

⊚ Beyond the Shmups: Choosing Your Games

OK, somehow you've gotten permission to take over the library (or part of it, at least) and turn it into a giant LAN party, and what's more you find that you have all of the required hardware, accessories, and power in order to pull off the event. How do you choose the games? This is an important question because while the most popular titles for LAN gaming are often shoot-'em-ups—or "shmups"—this genre is perhaps the least popular with parents and what we'll call the "concerned community" demographic, who is most likely to complain if the library sponsors an event for teens where all they do is shoot each other for several hours.

This isn't to say that one should immediately kowtow to censorship just because we're talking about violence in gaming, which is a hot-button topic in many circles. Because if we're serious about limiting the exposure of teens to violence and mature themes, why not attack YA literature or graphic novels or pretty much any other kind of material actively collected in the library stacks? No, I'm merely making it clear that shmups aren't the only kind of computer game that is fun to play in a LAN environment so that you can make the most informed choice for you, your community, and your circle of library stakeholders.

According to the online recommendation platform Slant, the five most popular LAN party PC games are as follows:

- Left 4 Dead 2—a two- to four-player co-op first-person shooter where the team is pitted against a zombie horde or two teams compete against each other (one human, one zombie).
- Age of Empires II HD—a real-time strategy game where players build their own empires based loosely on world history.
- Rocket League—a soccer game played with rocket-powered cars? 'Nuff said! It's fast, it's fun, and it's very addictive.
- Starcraft—another real-time strategy game, but this one is set in space. If you don't know what a Zerg Rush is, you're about to find out!
- Team Fortress 2—OK, this one is a legitimate shmup, but its colorful cartoonish characters (they have a YouTube channel with funny introductions and even more hilarious "Outtakes") and various game modes keep this venerable first-person shooter game—once called "the most fun you can have online" by *PC Gamer Magazine*—alive and kicking as a LAN classic!

Minecraft Is Its Own Beast

Wait a second—how can we talk about multiplayer online computer games and not mention Minecraft? While it is of course possible to configure the popular and addictive game for LAN play, Minecraft already has offline mode servers available so that it is not necessary to go to all of the trouble to network a bunch of machines locally. This having been said, however, Minecraft instead represents a shift from closed online gaming environments to a more open and networked gaming milieu. In some ways Minecraft behaves like a LAN game, but in others it is more like a massive multiplayer online (MMO) game or virtual world. Truly, Minecraft is in a category all its own!

I could easily fill an entire book with how to use Minecraft, but for the purpose of remaining within the scope of this chapter, let us focus on how to incorporate Minecraft into your library programming. Here are some of the considerations you'll want to take into account:

- Who will run the program? Will it be a library staff member or a volunteer from the community? If you are putting a library staff member in charge, remember that their presence in the gaming environment is no different than being assigned to the reference desk or any other library service point. The fact that Minecraft is a "game" should not obscure the fact that your staff member is representing your library at a virtual service point and that the work—even though it is facilitating play—should be considered work and respected as such in terms of scheduling priorities and other work considerations.

- Will you use the generic Minecraft game or MinecraftEdu? After acquiring Minecraft in 2014, Microsoft bought an educational variant of the game called MinecraftEdu in 2016 from a company called Teacher Gaming LLG and rechristened it Minecraft: Education Edition. This version of Minecraft is designed specifically for educational use (including use in a library setting) and adds settings and controls for classrooms, communication tools, and a tutorial for first-time educators.
- Will you run the program on a LAN or a server? If you wish to keep your Minecraft environment limited to your local area network, basically what will happen is that your facilitator will start their game and click on the "Open to LAN" button in order to allow others on the network to join that world. Although this is a fairly easy way to get started with running a Minecraft program at your library, it comes with some distinct disadvantages. First, when the person running the program logs off, the game goes with them. This form of shared LAN world also doesn't support the customization options available to dedicated Minecraft servers that are very popular in "modding" communities. Finally, the more people who log in and try to join via the local area network, the more the entire system will lag, as a networked series of computers are still only as fast as the underlying hardware.
- Will you pay for a remote server or host your own? If you do decide to go with a server, will you rent space or will you maintain your own local server? The basic trade-off here is cost for convenience—by opting for a paid hosting solution, you are paying a little extra so that you don't have to worry about the technical details of running your own server. This is probably a good option if you have little or zero IT support for your project. On the other hand, if you have good IT buy-in, you may want to experiment with hosting your own server, as it opens up even more options for customization with different server software available for download depending on exactly how adventurous and DIY you are actually feeling.
- Will you allow your library community online access to your server 24/7, or will you restrict access based on staff/volunteer availability? This is as much of a resource allocation question as it is one of basic trust. Although it is possible to design an online environment that is mostly safe most of the time, even the best-cultivated virtual world will nevertheless let in someone who will not respect your terms of service. If staff is always on hand to keep these rogue elements in order, then the potential impact of any one troll or griefer is lessened significantly. If you are allowing unsupervised online remote access to your server, however, then you will need to make it clear where and when the library's responsibilities begin and end.

The most important consideration for any would-be Minecraft librarian, however, is simply to join in the fun and play with your community. As John Blyberg, assistant director at the Darien Library in Darien, Connecticut, correctly observes: "The more you are online with your players, the more you will get to know them, their personalities, and their building style. They will begin to know you better—and form a radically different kind of relationship with your library, and with each other" (Blyberg 2015).

⦿ Roblox—Minecraft Meets LEGO Meets . . . Second Life?

Minecraft is the MMO gaming phenomenon that you've heard of—Roblox, on the other hand, is one that you may not know about, although your children almost certainly do.

Started in 2004 as an online 3-D physics modeling platform called DynaBlocks, Roblox officially launched in 2006 and ten years later boasts a community of thirty million active monthly users. What is Roblox? It's a sandbox game where players can create their own online games using the platform's proprietary engine and the Lua scripting language. Once they've created these games, they can explore the online virtual world to play others' games and try to entice other people to come and play theirs. Roblox even has its own online currency, Robux, which can be used to pay for goods and services in the game and even be exchanged for actual real-world money.

If this is starting to sound vaguely familiar, you're not alone—just as Second Life emerged onto the online scene in early 2003 much to the raves and plaudits of the digerati, who hailed it as the future of online social interaction, only to crash and burn when it fell short of delivering on its promises, many industry wags are now looking at Roblox as a potential rival to Minecraft itself. Indeed, there are many interesting similarities between Second Life and Roblox—the focus on user-created worlds and environments, the ability to make real-world money on virtual creative work, and the emphasis on games and gameplay. But whereas Second Life was more about social gaming and role-playing, Roblox emphasizes physics-based and arcade-style gameplay in a wacky "no holds barred" kind of universe where anything is possible. Erik Cassel, co-founder and former vice president of engineering at Roblox, "said he joined the Roblox team so that one day he would see someone drop a house into a giant blender in the game, and it happened. 'I love to write code, but it's the amazingly fun stuff that the ROBLOX community creates and does that motivates me. ROBLOX would be nothing without it'" (Fennimore 2017).

The other critical important difference is in the demographics. Whereas Second Life was created as a virtual world for adults and creators Linden Labs in fact struggled too late after the fact to meet the demands of teen users for a similar online environment, Roblox has actively courted not only teens but younger demographics as well, crafting a system of word whitelists and other social filters to prevent access to objectionable language and content. In fact, it was when children were playing the game that the creators of Roblox realized that their platform had multiplayer potential—when the kids started stacking blocks on each other's avatars! Indeed, children have been a huge factor in the amazing growth of Roblox, with much of its advertising being viral in nature, consisting of videos of gameplay on YouTube and other video-sharing platforms.

Another factor in Roblox's success has been the ease of access to the platform. Instead of being a paid game requiring massive downloads, updates, and patches to run properly, Roblox simply requires you to log in to its servers from virtually any kind of computer—PCs, tablets, and/or smartphones—and you're up and running after a brief installation or update. The lightweight nature of the Roblox app makes it easy for kids who don't necessarily have dedicated computers of their own to log in and jump back into the action quickly.

So what, if any, should be a gaming librarian's response to a potential Minecraft upstart such as Roblox? Should libraries try to build a presence in Roblox and other MMOs just as they did when Second Life was the Next Big Thing? It's hard to know how to answer these questions. First of all, there are only so many hours in the day, and keeping up with everything is an impossibility. However, it does not hurt to try to keep abreast of major trends in the video gaming world as they occur—for example, take the unlikely runaway success of Pokémon GO, which we will take a closer look at in the next chapter.

Key Points

- Although it is generally assumed that the library community isn't interested in console gaming or console games "because they already have them," the evidence indicates that roughly only half of all American households own one console system.
- The gaming market is sufficiently fragmented that libraries could help assume some of the risk of investing and involve themselves more actively in gamers' advisory.
- The PlayStation 4 currently dominates the consumer market—public libraries should consider investing in a PS4 or a Nintendo Switch due to popularity (total market) and popular demand (Switch is always sold out).
- Libraries could do more with curated PC gaming by making better use of a library Steam account and public terminals.
- LAN parties are still a great way to bring out the younger demographics, and there are many nonviolent popular LAN titles to play as well.
- Is Minecraft a unique phenomenon, or will other interactive virtual worlds (such as Roblox) eventually challenge it for supremacy?

References

Blyberg, John. 2015. "Our Public Library Minecraft Community." *School Library Journal*, April 3. www.slj.com/2015/04/technology/my-public-library-minecraft-community.

Entertainment Software Association. 2017. "Essential Facts About the Computer and Video Game Industry." *Entertainment Software Association* (website). www.theesa.com/about-esa/essential-facts-computer-video-game-industry (accessed January 2, 2018).

Fennimore, Jack. 2017. "Roblox: 5 Fast Facts You Need to Know." *Heavy*, July 12. heavy.com/games/2017/07/roblox-youtube-free-download-corporation-baszucki-cassel-nerfmodder/.

Harding-Rolls, Piers. 2017. "Market Insight: Sony Dominates 2016 Console Market With 57% Share of World Market Value." *IHS Markit* (blog), March 16. technology.ihs.com/590493/sony-dominates-2016-console-market-with-57-share-of-world-market-value.

Hoenke, Justin. 2013a. "Why I Bought an Original 1981 Ms. Pac Man Arcade Machine for My Library." *Medium*, June 27. medium.com/@justinlibrarian/why-i-bought-an-original-1981-ms-pac-man-arcade-machine-for-my-library-347cf9d79609.

———. 2013b. "#historyread and a Ms. Pac-Man Arcade Machine." *Read Watch Play* (blog), September 18. readwatchplay.wordpress.com/2013/09/18/historyread-and-a-ms-pac-man-arcade-machine/.

CHAPTER 8

How to Support Pokémon GO and Other Augmented Reality Games at Your Library

IN THIS CHAPTER

▷ From April Fool's to Killer App

▷ "Why Bother?" or Learning Lessons for the Next Big Thing

▷ Pokémon GO and Transmedia Literacy

▷ Pokémon GO 101: A Primer

▷ "A Wild Librarian Appears!": Librarians and Pokémon GO

▷ What Comes Next? The Future of Augmented Reality in the Library

From April Fool's to Killer App

A FUNNY THING HAPPENED TO THE WORLD of mobile computing in the summer of 2016—instead of sitting around being glued to their smartphones, kids (as well as teens, adults, and even seniors) were running all over their neighborhoods and beyond, roaming far and wide in search of parks, historical markers, and other places and buildings of interest in their community. Why? Because they were on the hunt for Pokémon, using their mobile devices in order to play Pokémon GO, the first breakaway hit game for smartphones using augmented reality. Pokémon GO may have been the first of its kind, but it almost certainly won't be the last—in this chapter we will look at the phenomenon of Pokémon GO, how libraries have embraced it, and what we can do to set ourselves up to anticipate and support future augmented reality games as librarians.

Believe it or not, Pokémon GO began as a 2014 April Fool's Day prank with Google (a company with a track record for this kind of humor), who announced that a new application called "Pokémon Challenge" would soon be released. The demand was so great for this imaginary product, however, that a company ultimately stepped in and fulfilled consumers' desires: Niantic, Inc., née Niantic Labs, which was an offshoot of an internal startup at Google, would take the reins and be responsible for creating the most downloaded mobile game in history. Released in July 2016, Pokémon GO has been downloaded more than 750 million times. At the peak of its popularity, Pokémon GO had as many as 21 million daily active users; even a year later, the augmented reality game still boasted 5 million daily active users and 65 million monthly active users. The average Pokémon GO player spends about twenty-six minutes a day playing the game, and thanks to a partially monetized system, Pokémon GO generated more than $950 million in revenue in 2016. Although the initial enthusiasm for the game may have waned, Niantic revamped Pokémon GO over the spring of 2017, with new features and enhancements to lure former devotees back to their Pokémon-chasing ways.

"Why Bother?" or Learning Lessons for the Next Big Thing

So if Pokémon GO is no longer as popular as it was in 2016, why should we spend time talking about it here in this book? The first and most important thing you should know about chasing library fads is that you will always be at least a cycle or two behind—this is especially so if you are trying to write a book about a cutting-edge library topic, where things are literally changing on a day-to-day basis. Once you acknowledge this basic truth, you quickly understand that even if the library world has moved on to the Next Big Thing, there are lessons to be learned every time you try to implement something new at your institution. Earlier in this book, I mentioned the importance of taking the time to evaluate and assess your attempts at innovation, but you could just as well apply that mandate to what you don't try to do as well. Did your library get caught up in the Pokémon GO hype? Why or why not? If you did, do you think it was worth the time and energy? If not, do you think your library missed out on an opportunity to engage patrons in a new and exciting way?

Pokémon GO may have been a singular phenomenon, but all signs point to it merely being the first of a veritable onslaught of augmented reality games and applications, many of which are currently in the final phases of development. If we are obligated as librarians to meet our patrons' expectations for supporting new technologies as they purchase and adopt them, surely by examining Pokémon GO more closely, we are preparing ourselves not just for the current best-selling augmented reality game but what is to come as well.

Pokémon GO and Transmedia Literacy

If we want to dig a little deeper, however, Amanda Hovious—a librarian and instructional designer who writes the blog Designer Librarian—writes that Pokémon GO is a perfect example of a twenty-first-century learning tool:

1. It's a fun way to practice **critical thinking and problem solving skills**. Pokemon Go requires strategic thinking, and strategic thinking is central to successful problem solving.
2. It's **collaborative**. 21st century learning is all about collaboration, and Pokemon Go fosters a sense of teamwork, something so important to the collaborative process.
3. It requires **information literacy skills**. Finding, evaluating, and synthesizing information coming from both the virtual and physical world is information literacy in practice.
4. It promotes **spatial thinking skills**. With the explosion and increasing ubiquity of GIS technology, spatial thinking is an essential skill for 21st century learning. And spatial thinking is an important skill in STEM education.
5. It's an avenue to **digital citizenship**. Digital literacy, digital access, digital commerce (pokecoins), digital etiquette (and real world etiquette), and digital security (personal information) are just some of the elements that must be practiced or addressed during Pokemon Go play. (Hovious, 2016)

Hovious also emphasizes the fact that Pokémon GO is a very successful form of transmedia storytelling and as such should be of great interest to librarians beyond any ephemeral interest in the game itself or the hype surrounding it. This is a very interesting point, for surely one of the reasons the Pokémon GO app was so successful was the fact that, unlike its augmented reality game predecessors, it was based on an extremely popular existing intellectual property that was already rich with multimedia content—a preexisting shared universe, if you will. That universe suddenly could be projected into the real world and played with just as patrons can play the Pokémon handheld or console video games or collectible trading card game, watch the various TV shows, or read the books.

This notion of immersive world-building is an important theme in transmedia literacy, and it will become increasingly imperative for librarians to address programmatically as this new form of storytelling matures and evolves. From a transmedia literacy perspective, Pokémon GO becomes as important a part of this "expanded universe" of intellectual properties as it is just being a game in its own right. This is where you run into some truly thought-provoking questions: should games like Pokémon GO be "collected" by the library like the other elements of this transmedia storytelling franchise? And if so, how do we accomplish this in terms of access, discovery, and long-term preservation? While a thorough discussion of these concerns is well beyond the scope of this book, we should at the very least keep in mind that these are conversations we as librarians will increasingly find ourselves in the middle of, whether we are prepared to have them or not.

Pokémon GO 101: A Primer

As mentioned previously, Pokémon GO is what's known as an augmented reality (or AR) game, where virtual information is overlaid onto real-world locations. In order to speed up the development process for Pokémon GO, Niantic used geolocation from its previous AR game, called Ingress, which converted real-world locations into either PokéStops or PokéGyms. PokéStops were basically caches that players could visit periodically in order to acquire the necessary supplies for hunting Pokémon—such as PokéBalls, which the player "throws" at the Pokémon by flicking them across the screen of their smartphone—and PokéGyms were places where players could train their Pokémon and battle each other by proxy in order to try and claim the facility on behalf of their faction (Team Valor,

Team Mystic, or Team Instinct). Although the previous AR game Ingress allowed places such as businesses to either add or remove themselves from the list of geolocation results, when Pokémon GO launched, it did not permit the owners of locations this functionality and is still working on enabling it at the time of writing this book.

This is particularly unfortunate for institutions that were eager to get involved with the Pokémon GO phenomenon but were not included in the original geolocation data as either PokéStops or PokéGyms. However, there are often practical workarounds. For example, although the Westport Library itself does not register as a PokéStop or PokéGym, two sculptures on its property show up as PokéStops, and there are several additional PokéStops adjacent to the library building as well. This allowed the library to incorporate these locations in a kind of virtual scavenger hunt to supplement existing programming, such as a storybook walk that passed by several of these PokéStops along the way. The lack of an adjacent PokéGym, however, was not as easily overcome and highlights the double-edged nature of augmented reality games and other similar applications.

When one is not necessarily tethered to one's real location, you have the ability to browse real-world locations with a greater deal of freedom; whereas if you are playing a game that insists on a strict 1:1 geolocation, not only are you at the mercy of the location itself but also the accuracy of the original mapmakers and compilers of the geocoding data. People who live in cities can swing a cat and hit not just one but several PokéStops or PokéGyms—some apartment-dwellers merely need to change rooms in the house to access these different geolocated features. Compare that to the plight of the suburban or rural Pokémon hunter/trainer, where such features are few and far between. Granted, Pokémon GO attempts to make up for this disparity by incentivizing walking as the primary way to hatch Pokémon eggs, but this will continue to be a challenge for augmented reality: how do you craft an augmented reality experience that is fun for everyone when reality itself is not equitably distributed?

◎ "A Wild Librarian Appears!": Librarians and Pokémon GO

While libraries cannot solve any problems presented by geography, they can enhance their patrons' experience playing Pokémon GO in ways that can make the library a more welcoming and attractive venue for this community. For example, many locations—both businesses and non-for-profit and/or cultural institutions—have embraced their status as a PokéStop or PokéGym and used this information as part of their own PR and outreach to lure more customers to their place. As a further enticement, places that are PokéStops can make their locations more likely to produce Pokémon by installing or "dropping" a Lure Module onto the PokéStop. These lures will attract additional and more rare varieties of Pokémon for thirty minutes while it is in use and moreover are a benefit to anyone within range of the PokéStop (unlike Incense, which functions in a similar fashion to Lure Modules, except that they only work for the individual using the item). Since a Lure Module costs one hundred PokéCoins—or roughly one dollar in real-world currency—the cost of keeping all of your PokéStops outfitted with Lures at all times could become rather expensive, so just like a bar or restaurant might drop some Lures around lunchtime or happy hour, it is recommended that libraries use Lure Modules strategically so as to coincide with other activities that might be of interest to the patrons who are being "Lured" into the library, such as teen programming or a MakerSpace event.

Libraries can also further leverage their roles if they are PokéGyms or PokéStops with additional programming and outreach efforts. The Bluffton Library in Bluffton, South Carolina—which also happened to be a PokéGym—decided to welcome all of the new traffic coming in through their doors by setting up a display that recognized whenever the PokéGym changed hands. Kids and teens were encouraged to let someone at the service desk know when they managed to win the gym for their faction so the librarians could change the colors on the display, which also contained a curated selection of Pokémon books, DVDs, and other media (Cawthon 2016). Other libraries held events where library staff would conduct guided tours of the local PokéGyms and PokéStops. For example, the Mentor Public Library in Mentor, Ohio, held a walking tour of Pokémon GO features adjacent to their Lake Branch Library, which they billed a "Pokémon Safari," culminating in a visit to a PokéGym where patrons could try and take over the gym for their respective factions (Mentor Public Library 2016). Even more ambitious, the Baltimore County Library System in Baltimore, Maryland, held "Poke Crawls," where they would lead groups of patrons on a tour of all nineteen library branches in the county (Pacella 2016). Similar safaris, crawls, or tours have been offered by other libraries. Some libraries have put these tours to dual-use—for example, introducing the campus to new students in the case of academic libraries or the surrounding neighborhood for public libraries. In both cases it is a clever outreach tactic, using the library as the go-between for the library community and the "real" world outside the library's doorstep, as well as setting itself up as the potential intermediary for any related programs or activities that may result from these outreach efforts.

Another way librarians engaged their Pokémon-hunting patrons was to encourage them to hunt Pokémon not just in and around their buildings but right in the library stacks as well. An interesting feature of the Pokémon GO app is that players can choose to hunt their Pokémon in "AR" mode, which overlays the Pokémon against a live image from your smartphone's camera (turning off AR mode disables the camera and allows the player to hunt against a simple green generic backdrop). As a result, players can take pictures of the Pokémon they are hunting while at the same time featuring the place where they are hunting, which can then be posted online and shared via social media. Many enterprising businesses and other organizations caught on to the potential quickly and asked their customers or patrons to share pictures of the Pokémon they "caught" on their premises.

To this end, the New York Public Library invited patrons to explore the stacks while they hunted for rare and elusive Pokémon, posting pictures of Pokémon that library staff had caught in various iconic locations of the library and encouraging patrons to submit tagged pictures of their own catches as well (Weiss 2016). The Anne Arundel County Public Library actually went a step further and created a "PokeDex" display for the library, which featured a running tally of all of the Pokémon caught within the library, based on the pictures patrons brought in (Compendium News Staff 2016). At the Westport Library, for example, we tied Pokémon hunting to our Giant Annual Book Sale in July 2016, challenging shoppers to find as many Pokémon as they could while they were looking for bargain books, DVDs, and other items for sale (Woog 2016).

Finally, many libraries crafted their own programming to supplement the Pokémon GO craze and tie it into existing library services and initiatives, often in conjunction with the children's or teen librarians or the library MakerSpace. Many libraries, for example, already have an active Pokémon collectible card gaming program in place or were inspired by the Pokémon GO phenomenon to start one at their library.

The aforementioned Mentor Public Library created a system of Pokémon-themed trainer badges that could be earned by completing certain library tasks:

For the Boulder Badge, tell a librarian about your favorite book.
For the Cascade Badge, play our Who's that Pokémon challenge.
For the Thunder Badge, show us your highest-level Pokémon.
For the Rainbow Badge, check out a fiction book.
For the Soul Badge, it's Quiz Time! Go ask a librarian for a question.
For the Marsh Badge, find a book about somewhere that you'd like to visit.
For the Volcano Badge, show us a screenshot of a Pokémon that you caught at the library.
(Yes, we're a PokéStop, and you never know when we're going to drop a lure.)
For the Earth Badge, find Mewtwo in the library and tell a librarian what he's saying.
(Mentor Public Library 2016)

Kids could earn two badges per week and would win a prize if they earned all eight.

At the Westport Library, we offered a weeklong series of sewing classes where library patrons could create their own Pokémon costumes for Halloween with a local freelance theatrical costumer (Westport Library 2016). The Anne Arundel County Library (which we also mentioned earlier in this chapter) offered a Pikachu bracelet crafting activity as well. The Public Library of Mount Vernon and Knox County enlisted their MakerSpace's button-making machine to create Fingerprint Pokémon Buttons, where teens cleverly transformed their fingerprints into various Pokémon and then pressed them into buttons (Jensen 2016). At the Perry Public Library in Perry, Ohio, patrons were encouraged to come in and measure themselves to compare their height with that of various Pokémon, an offshoot of a similar activity involving superheroes that they had done in the previous year. This activity proved overwhelmingly popular not just with children and teens but adults as well, all of whom were fascinated to come see how they "measured up" to their favorite Pokémon creatures (Jensen 2016).

What Comes Next? The Future of Augmented Reality in the Library

We have already mentioned that Pokémon GO may be the first augmented reality application to break through into mainstream commercial success with the general public, but it certainly won't be the last: as we speak, there are myriad new AR games and apps in development as businesses scramble to capitalize on the immense popularity of Pokémon GO and its massive financial opportunities. One such game is Snatch (www.snatchhq .com), a "free to play virtual treasure hunt" where players use their smartphones to locate parcels hidden in augmented reality. Not only do some of the parcels contain real-world prizes, such as vacations, concert tickets, other rewards, or even money, but players can actually "snatch" these parcels from one another (hence the name of the game), putting an interesting player versus player spin on the game. Snatch was introduced in the United Kingdom in 2016 and launched in the United States in 2017.

If shooting other people sounds more fun to you than snatching their stuff, then you might be interested in Father.IO (www.indiegogo.com/projects/father-io-massive -multiplayer-laser-tag-app#), a game that bills itself as the "world's first real-life, massive multiplayer, first person shooter." An Indiegogo startup, Father.IO combines your smartphone with a plug-in "Inceptor," a keychain-sized piece of hardware that functions exactly like a wearable laser tag gun and harness. Players engage with one another using the camera of their smartphones, which layer tactical information and other useful gameplay data onto a heads-up augmented reality display. There is also a strategic, real-world map-based companion game using the Father.IO app where players capture territory for their factions and exploit it for valuable in-game resources.

To gain a better understanding of Pokémon GO itself, it might be worth taking a second look at Ingress (www.ingress.com), Niantic Labs' first attempt at an augmented reality game and the basic framework for the Pokémon GO app. On the simplest of levels, both Ingress and Pokémon GO involve exploring the real world in order to unlock materials and support through the augmented reality interface, but whereas Pokémon GO's gameplay is mostly solitary in nature and focused on individual achievement, Ingress is a game played both tactically and strategically at the same time, as players compete not just to "win" stations for their faction but to complete triangles of faction-owned stations on the map, a process which can only be done in concert with other faction members when the other points of the triangle can be hundreds of miles or more away. Pokémon GO players who lament the game's shortcomings often point to Ingress as an example of what it could have or should have been—if nothing else, Ingress definitely feels more developed and is worth a look to see what a future AR game might feature.

That being said, one might not want to count out Niantic Labs and Pokémon GO quite yet: although the amount of new users has steadily dropped since 2016's whirlwind launch, an online survey in June 2017 showed that Pokémon GO still had a steady base of users who played the game every day (Chan 2017). Meanwhile, Niantic continues to add new gameplay features—including raids, in which players can team up in order to defeat super-powered "Raid Bosses"—as well as more Pokémon to be hunted, caught, and trained so as to entice both new users and previous Pokémon GO players who lost interest in the game over time.

Perhaps it will be some time yet before another AR game is able to dethrone Pokémon GO. A 2016 article in *Rolling Stone* argues that Pokémon GO's wild success was as much about the Pokémon phenomenon as a whole as it was about the new smartphone app:

> What's clear is that you don't get Pokémon Go without the underlying tech, but you don't get a phenomenon without the Pokémon brand. "Pokémon is a singularly powerful and beloved brand," says Loeb when asked to predict how soon we'll start to see clones of the game. "It will be nearly impossible for anyone to reproduce this success. That means developers will need to be creative to try to get into the space being pioneered by this game. In short: I don't think we'll see a slew of direct clones. Or, maybe we will, but I don't think they will do well." (*Rolling Stone* 2016)

In other words, if a rival developer truly wishes to attain the same level of frenzy with the public that Pokémon GO achieved, they will need to exploit a similarly beloved intellectual property. This brings us back to the beginning of this chapter with our discussion about the growing importance of transmedia literacy, as it is clear here that at least for the time being our fascination with augmented reality is part of a larger whole. Also, and perhaps even more interesting, is the notion that transmedia literacy itself can help introduce our community to other adjacent concepts—such as augmented reality and games.

⊚ Key Points

- Libraries and librarians still have a lot to learn about how to support "fad" programming such as Pokémon GO.
- Pokémon GO may represent the first of many augmented reality (AR) games and applications now that the gameplay concept has gone mainstream.
- Not only can transmedia literacy help us understand Pokémon GO as a phenomenon, but it may help us anticipate the needs of transmedia literacy for libraries and how these pressures differ from traditional literacy.
- Libraries that were most successful in programming embraced Pokémon GO players as peers and engaged them on the level of play.

⊚ References

Cawthon, Graham. 2016. "Local Library Goes Viral Thanks to Pokemon Plans." *The Island Packet*, July 13. www.islandpacket.com/news/local/article89386062.html.

Chan, Stephanie. 2017. "Survey Says: Pokémon Go's Loyal Fans Remain Everyday Players, Even as Craze Dies Down." *VentureBeat*, July 6. venturebeat.com/2017/07/06/survey-says -pokemon-gos-loyal-fans-remain-everyday-players-even-as-craze-dies-down.

Compendium News Staff. 2016. "'Catch Them All!' Pokémon Go and Your Library." *Compendium: News for Pennsylvania Libraries* (blog), August 16. compendium.ocl-pa.org/catch-them-all -pokemon-go-and-your-library/.

Hovious, Amanda. 2016. "5 Ways in Which Pokemon Go Exemplifies 21st Century Learning." *Designer Librarian* (blog), July 20. designerlibrarian.wordpress.com/2016/07/20/5-ways-in -which-pokemon-go-exemplifies-21st-century-learning.

Jensen, Karen. 2016. "MakerSpace: Making Fingerprint Pokemon Go Buttons." *School Library Journal*, July 25. www.teenlibrariantoolbox.com/2016/07/makerspace-making-finger print-pokemon-go-buttons.

Mentor Public Library. 2016. "Go Pokemon Hunting With Us at the Library." *Mentor Public Library* (website). www.mentorpl.org/go-pokemon-hunting-with-us-at-the-library (accessed January 2, 2018).

Pacella, Rachel. 2016. "County Libraries Use Pokemon Go to Attract Patrons." *The Baltimore Sun*, July 23. www.baltimoresun.com/news/maryland/baltimore-county/towson/ph-tt-pokemon -crawl-0722-20160723-story.html.

Rolling Stone. 2016. "Why We Won't See More Games Like 'Pokemon Go.'" *Rolling Stone*, July 19. www.rollingstone.com/culture/news/why-we-wont-see-more-games-like-pokemon -go-w429840.

Weiss, Lauren. 2016. "Catching 'Em All at NYPL with Pokémon GO." *New York Public Library* (website), July 8. www.nypl.org/blog/2016/07/08/catching-em-all-nypl-pokemon-go.

Westport Library. 2016. "Create Your Own Pokemon-ster Pokemon Costume Workshop." *Westport Library* (website). westportlibrary.org/events/create-your-own-pokemon-ster-pokemon -costume-workshop (accessed January 2, 2018).

Woog, Dan. 2016. "Weedles, Zubats, Ekans and More: Pokemon Go Floods Westport." *06880: Where Westport Meets the World* (blog), July 14. 06880danwoog.com/2016/07/14/weedles -zubats-ekans-and-more-pokemon-go-floods-westport.

CHAPTER 9

Role-Playing Games in the Library

━━━━━━━━━━━━━━━ **IN THIS CHAPTER** ━━━━━━━━━━━━━━━

▷ From your Parents' Basement to the Library

▷ RPGs: A Very Short History

▷ How to Ensure a Critical Hit: Best Practices for Your Library RPG Event

▷ D&D and Beyond: Choosing the Right RPG for Your Library

▷ Fantasy: Pathfinder and Other Options

▷ Cthul-WHO? Horror Role-Playing Games for the Library

▷ Other Genres, Other Worlds

▷ *Mad Max: Fury Road* with Funny Dice

▷ The Shattered Frontier, the Weird West, and the Dogs in the Vineyard: Wild West RPGs

▷ Role-Playing in the Matrix: Cyberpunk RPGs

▷ From Science Fiction to Space Opera: Sci-Fi RPGs

▷ Batgirl Was a Librarian: Superhero RPGs

▷ How About a Nice Dungeons & Dragons Board Game Instead?

▷ Not Just for Teens and Nostalgic Adults: RPGs for Kids

A handful of polyhedral dice from Dungeons & Dragons.

⊚ From Your Parents' Basement to the Library

ROLE-PLAYING GAMES (OR RPGS) ARE a quintessential form of library gaming programming. Not only are they collaborative forms of storytelling where players are encouraged to resolve challenges as a group using their imagination and a handful of polyhedral dice, but they also embrace the Maker and DIY movements by encouraging players to supplement their "theater of the mind" action with painted miniatures and fantastic battlegrounds, from dank dungeons to medieval castles to bustling cityscapes. Role-playing games are also heavily textual, as each game usually comes with a core rulebook and myriad other supplements or "splatbooks" that help fill out the game's narrative universe and give players various options for customizing their characters; the authors of these rulebooks may also suggest additional reading for inspiration or encourage players to do their own research when role-playing during historical periods. Finally, running a successful role-playing game requires a good space that is accommodating for a group of up to a dozen players but intimate enough so that the players can immerse themselves in the action without disturbing anyone else—and vice versa.

If someone were to imagine a new type of game from scratch explicitly designed to maximize its potential affinity with libraries, they would be hard-pressed to come up with something more library-friendly than role-playing games. Nevertheless, with a few noteworthy exceptions, RPGs are still only rarely found in libraries. Why the disconnect? While some portion of our ambivalence toward role-playing games is part of the broader uncertainty about incorporating games and gaming into the library, we must also account for the mixed reception RPGs have received from the general public thanks to the efforts of pop culture watchdogs and other self-appointed moral guardians in the 1980s, who linked D&D to Satanism, occult worship, and other forms of antisocial behavior. Cartoonist and evangelical fundamentalist Christian gadfly Jack Chick even dedicated one of his infamous Chick Tracts to the dangers of Dungeons & Dragons, "exposing" it as a recruitment tool for Satanists and other demon-worshippers. This moral panic reached its apogee in 1982 with the made-for-television movie *Mazes and Monsters* (starring Tom Hanks, no less), which was based on a sensationalized account of the death of a college student at Michigan State University that was allegedly linked to playing D&D.

Although the fear that Dungeons & Dragons was going to corrupt the youth ultimately subsided, the stigma attached to playing D&D would linger for decades; only recently has role-playing begun to emerge from this shadow, with many notable public figures—such as comedian Patton Oswalt, actor Vin Diesel, writer George R. R. Martin, and investor and entrepreneur Alexis Ohanian—all embracing their geeky identity as former or even current Dungeons & Dragons players. D&D and role-playing games in general have also benefited from the rise of nerd chic in popular culture, whereby once marginalized forms of genre entertainment such as fantasy, science fiction, and comic book superheroes have all entered into mainstream movies and television; meanwhile, board gaming is enjoying its own renaissance and video gamers have turned "e-sports" into a multi-billion dollar industry. Role-playing games couldn't find a more fertile environment for its own triumphant comeback.

As luck would have it, Dungeons & Dragons only recently came out with the fifth edition of its ruleset, providing a fresh but familiar entry point for both new players and old players who used to sling dice in their parents' basements back in the day. This also offers a rare opportunity for libraries to incorporate role-playing games into your library's gaming programming. In this chapter I will show you how to set up a role-playing game program in your library, including how to choose the right RPG for your library, whether or not to collect RPG rulebooks as part of your library's collections, and ways that you can leverage the renewed interest in D&D and other RPGs into other MakerSpace or teen activities such as 3-D printing, DIY crafting, and storytelling.

◎ RPGs: A Very Short History

First, however, let us take a closer look at the unique history of role-playing games, as by understanding where RPGs come from, we will get a better sense of how they fit into the spectrum of gaming activities and related hobbies. Although the antecedents of improvisational role-play date back at least as far as the commedia dell'arte in sixteenth-century Italy, if not earlier, the tactical predecessor of role-playing games evolved from the rules for miniature war gaming. *Chainmail, or Rules for Medieval Miniatures* was published in 1971 by war gamers Gary Gygax and Jeff Perren as a way to allow for players to take control of individual soldiers and make them behave in unconventional ways that traditional war gaming rules could not anticipate or properly adjudicate. *Chainmail* also included rules for introducing fantastic elements into the game, such as magical effects, so that if you wanted to re-create the Battle of Agincourt with French wizards throwing fireballs at the English longbowmen, you could now resolve this and see who would prevail.

As the emphasis of gameplay continued to shift from the group to the individual, Dave Arneson and Gygax responded with expanded editions and supplements to the *Chainmail* ruleset, fleshing out the concept of the player as character with rules for classes, experience points, and improving characters incrementally by level progression. This new ruleset, dubbed "The Fantasy Game," was published as Dungeons & Dragons (or D&D) in 1974. It proved to be enormously popular among the war gamer community and spread quickly to college and high school students so that by 1981 there were more than three million people playing D&D across the United States, Canada, and the United Kingdom. (The first officially licensed French translation was in 1982; since then the game has been translated into many other foreign languages, with the fifth edition rulebooks being released simultaneously in French, German, Italian, Japanese, Spanish, Polish, and Portuguese.)

By 2004, Dungeons & Dragons could boast having more than twenty million players and more than a billion dollars in sales, although by this time D&D had to compete for time, money, and attention with a burgeoning video gaming market and myriad competitors—including World of Darkness, which featured vampires and werewolves instead of Tolkienesque elves and dwarves; GURPS (General Universal Role-Playing System), which allowed players to have adventures in virtually any genre they chose; and independent RPG systems such as Dogs in the Vineyard, which emphasized the morally ambiguous dimensions of role-playing over the fantasy trope of epic quests. These centrifugal forces impacted the RPG community such that even though Dungeons & Dragons was still the *primus inter pares*, there was no one definitive role-playing system that all players could share in common—even the D&D players themselves would cleave to their favorite editions even long after they were no longer being officially supported by TSR or Wizards of the Coast. (I, for example, am a diehard second edition fan, as this is the version of Dungeons & Dragons I was playing in high school and college; this officially makes me what gamers call a "grognard.") An actual competing fantasy role-playing system—Pathfinder—spun off from the third edition of D&D as its own separate entity. The RPG tabletop market seemed to be permanently fractured and on its way to being supplanted slowly but surely by the role-playing genre of video games, which keep getting more interactive and immersive with each new release.

Then, in 2014, something extraordinary happened: riding on a tidal wave of nostalgia and angry gamers who felt frustrated and disenfranchised by the rule changes of the fourth edition, owners Wizards of the Coast released the fifth edition of the game after an exhaustive period of both open and closed playtesting meant to recapture old D&D enthusiasts while at the same time captivate a brand new generation of fantasy role-playing gamers. With sales of the core rulebooks having gone through several successful print runs—according to lead designer Mike Mearls, the fifth edition *Player's Handbook* has outsold every previous edition of the game—three years after its initial publication the D&D *Player's Handbook* is still in the Top 100 of all Amazon book sales (at the time of this book's writing it was ranked at #90). Suddenly Dungeons & Dragons appears to be everywhere, with ubiquitous references in television shows such as *The Big Bang Theory, Community*—which devoted an entire episode to the cast of the show playing the game—and of course the cult hit Netflix series *Stranger Things*, in which D&D played a critical role.

Part of this renaissance is attributable to the fact that, as mentioned before, the stigma of role-playing games that lingered over several generations of gamers is no longer there, especially with playing Dungeons & Dragons while growing up being hailed as the secret to the success of many talented individuals not just in the entertainment business but in practically every other industry as well, as the social skill set required to play D&D is remarkably similar to the soft skills that are in such great demand in today's managerial workplace. Finally, whereas the barrier to entry for role-playing games was always somewhat daunting, with the need to find a group looking for players or to convince your own circle of friends to take up the hobby, the game itself has been demystified and made more accessible by the Internet. Players looking for groups now can use Meetup or myriad other online services, many of which—such as Roll20—allow players to join live D&D or other role-playing games via webcam. Also, even those who can't find a group at the moment or don't have time for a regular time commitment can now eavesdrop on other RPG groups as they livestream their sessions on Twitch or other online game-streaming services. With so many options to play or watch Dungeons & Dragons, it's no wonder that, even in its fifth iteration, the game is alive and well among gamers and that other role-playing games continue to find new and receptive audiences as well.

ⓖ How to Ensure a Critical Hit: Best Practices for Your Library RPG Event

Although there any many role-playing games to choose from—and we will take a brief whirlwind tour of the various RPG genres in the sections below—there are several universal aspects to role-playing games that allow us to suggest a series of best practices for hosting an RPG event at your library. Let's take a look at them now.

1. Space and noise. Role-playing games require the proper combination of breathing space and acoustics. Bearing in mind that most RPG sessions can last for three or more hours, you want to make sure that your players have enough personal space so that they do not become uncomfortable after prolonged periods of being crammed into the same room with several other people. At the same time, you need to make sure that this space is not in a place where voices will carry inordinately. Role-playing isn't always about yelling and shouting, but it is louder than most other library activities. If your library patrons tend to complain about the noise in common spaces, you should be sure to find a location where if and when the players do get carried away by their enthusiasm, you don't have to worry about their enjoyment being a disturbance to other library users. Also, are you expecting guests or other walk-in participants for this event? If so, you will need an even larger space to accommodate the extended crowd of onlookers or players waiting for their own session. A word of caution about hosting multiple concurrent tables or RPG sessions in the same room, however—such a room can get very loud very fast, with the result that many people may have difficulty listening to their own session over the background din (this is a common complaint at gaming conferences, especially at overbooked events). If you have a larger space for multiple sessions, try to keep the tables as far away from each other as possible so as to minimize intrusive conversations from the other games.

2. Age and genre expectations. By their very nature, role-playing games tend to explore a lot of themes that some members of your library community might find objectionable. The last thing you want to do is deal with aggrieved parents who thought their children were going to play games at the library, not kill orcs or exorcise demons. It is vitally important therefore for you to overcommunicate the recommended ages and audiences for the RPGs that you will be featuring at your library gaming events. For example, Dungeons & Dragons has a casual "hack & slash" feel and might not be suitable for audiences under the age of thirteen; whereas a horror game like Call of Cthulhu might be an eighteen-plus event due to its graphic depictions of violence and treatment of extremist religious cults. While you may entertain exceptions to any of these recommendations, it might be better to offer RPG programming that would be more suited to younger audiences instead. At the end of this chapter, I will include a selection of role-playing games that are ideal for children—I hope that you will use these suggestions as a jumping-off point for your exploration into the relatively new but steadily growing market of kids' RPGs.

3. Is this a campaign, or is it a one-shot? Just like board games, RPGs can be played in a "one-shot" capacity—that is to say, the Gamemaster (GM) and players sit down for one session together only, with no continuation of previously existing characters or setting. One-shots are great ways to draw in new audience members or play for a group whose attendance might be spotty or unpredictable; one-shot sessions are also excellent for introducing new role-playing games, so that players don't feel the need to commit to an unfamiliar system or setting. If you are playing a campaign, try to remember that not all players may be able to attend on a week-to-week basis and that you may have both people who wish to drop out as well as those who may want to join after a campaign has officially started. Negotiating variable attendance is a headache for any GM, but a library-sponsored GM should try to err on the side of flexibility, as the goal is to promote a fun and welcoming atmosphere to all program attendees.

4. Time and frequency. It is difficult if not impossible to run an RPG session in anything less than a three- to four-hour block of time; many sessions can easily run for much longer. Be sure and make enough time in your schedule for your event so that your GM and players do not feel rushed to finish—this is especially true for "one-shot" RPG sessions. If your library closes at 9 p.m., for example, consider reserving a 5 p.m. to 9 p.m. time slot for your role-playing game program. Also you should determine how often you'd like to run a particular RPG event. Many external gaming groups often meet on some variation of a weekly or monthly schedule (for example, I currently belong to two RPG groups, each of which meets every other week). A weekly RPG gaming group represents a significant investment in time and resources, so unless there is enough demand to warrant running on a weekly basis, it is recommended that you start with a monthly or biweekly session and go from there.

5. Material resources. While it's always fun to buy and bring your own funny-looking dice, you should make sure that the library has enough of the essential materials for role-playing stocked on hand to ensure that nobody is excluded from participation because they don't have their own. This includes:

   a. A generous supply of dice, both in the six-sided variety (aka d6) and polyhedral sets, which include four-sided (d4), six-sided (d6), eight-sided (d8), ten-sided (d10), twelve-sided (d12), and twenty-sided dice (d20). Some RPGs, such as Shadowrun, require players to roll a large amount of six-sided dice at a time—fortunately most dice vendors sell 12mm d6's in blocks of thirty-six in a variety of colors and style.

   b. Some kind of surface for drawing maps and a supply of dry-erase markers and erasers. The ideal for this would be a laminated vinyl or plastic sheet with a grid of one-inch squares, as the 1 inch = 5 feet metric is standard for most role-playing games using miniatures. These kinds of surfaces are usually called "battle mats" and can be bought either at your friendly local game store or online. Depending on the RPG, you may also want to include battle mats with a hex grid as well. Hexagonal grids are often used for larger-scale maps, as they permit a wider range of movement.

   c. A base stock of miniatures. Although it is nice to have personalized miniatures for every player, the most important thing for gaming purposes is to have some kind of token to represent the player's position on a map, so even if a player does not have a mini of their own, they can choose from a collection of stock miniature figures. There are several RPG vendors that offer cheap generic minis; also, if your library has a 3-D printer, this is an excellent opportunity to print your own miniatures. More about miniatures, including painting them, will appear in chapter 11.

    d. Copies of the core rulebook and other key supplements. If the library is offering programming for a particular RPG, then it stands to reason that it should purchase at least one copy of the printed ruleset for the library's collection for use as an on-site reference for the GM and players. Whether you want to add additional circulating copies of the book would depend on local demand and your budget for gaming books. For more information, see the section below on collecting RPG rulebooks and other role-playing game materials.

6.   Human resources. Finally, you'll want to make sure that you have an experienced DM/GM available for every session that you schedule, as role-playing games are sufficiently complicated that it's hard to learn how to run a game as DM or GM on the fly while also ensuring that the players are all enjoying themselves as well. Does someone on your library staff already know how to run the RPG you'd like to feature? Or perhaps a volunteer? If no one at the library is able to serve as DM/GM, you may want to consider reaching out to your local friendly game store or recruiting someone online through Meetup or something similar. Whomever you end up choosing to run your RPG event, please be sure to remind them to be welcoming and inclusive as ambassadors of the library and always to err on the side of fun.

D&D and Beyond: Choosing the Right RPG for Your Library

Having spent a few pages talking about the history of Dungeons & Dragons and its importance to the history of role-playing games in general, one might get the erroneous impression that D&D is the only RPG worth running for a library gaming program. This would be a mistake, as there are many interesting role-playing games available on the market right now, each one with its particular strengths and weaknesses. Ideally you would want to choose an RPG that speaks to your community and their gaming interests. For example, the violence depicted in a standard session of D&D might be a little too much for a younger gaming group, or perhaps you have a group of teens who already get together to discuss horror and the supernatural who might enjoy a scary role-playing game instead; it's even possible that you may live in a community where Dungeons & Dragons is still viewed with some suspicion, so you may want to opt for an RPG based on *Star Wars* or science fiction. Here we will take a quick look at some possibilities for a range of genres that might be suitable for different audiences.

Fantasy: Pathfinder and Other Options

It is possible that your library gaming community is already familiar with Pathfinder, a system that grew out of the third edition of Dungeons & Dragons in 2008. At the time Wizards of the Coast was publishing the new version of D&D—also called the "d20 System"—under an Open Game License (OGL), which encouraged amateur, indie, and third-party authors to create and sell their own fantasy gaming materials using the core ruleset provided by Dungeons & Dragons. For Wizards of the Coast, this proved to be a double-edged sword, for although this did lead to an explosion of splatbooks, rules supplements, and other gaming publications, it also allowed for gamers dissatisfied with the current state of D&D to take what the OGL allowed them to and form their own competing fantasy role-playing system called Pathfinder.

So when should you choose Pathfinder over Dungeons & Dragons for your library gaming group?

1. If you have someone willing to run the game (more about this later) who is more familiar with Pathfinder than D&D.
2. If you have a majority of players who grew up playing third edition D&D or the d20 system.
3. If you have a gaming group that enjoys a system that emphasizes having a rule for every contingency and is relatively complex.
4. If your gaming group would like to play fantasy role-playing in a setting based on something other than generic Western Late Middle Ages.
5. If you are looking for an RPG with excellent PDF book support—currently Pathfinder has PDF copies of all of its texts for sale, whereas Wizards of the Coast does not sell ebook versions of their D&D rulebooks.

Much of this is gross oversimplification, as both systems are popular and beloved and stand up on their own merits, but the gist of Pathfinder is that rather than radically changing the ruleset as fourth edition D&D did, it continued to evolve and expand on the third edition and thus feels like a more "complete" system, whereas this latest iteration of Dungeons & Dragons is easy to pick up and has that epic old-school fantasy role-playing feel to it, but it's still finding its way. Hopefully a combination of the factors above will help you choose one system over the other.

At the risk of making your choice even more complicated, there are a couple of other viable fantasy role-playing systems that you may want to choose as well: Savage Worlds and Dungeon World. Savage Worlds, first published in 2003, is actually a set of generic role-playing rules that emphasize action and speed of play over all other considerations. The result is something akin to playing in the setting of a "pulp" novel from the late nineteenth or early twentieth century and provides a snappy departure from both D&D and Pathfinder, making Savage Worlds a great option for one-shot adventures. Dungeon World is an interesting variation in its own right, as the system allows the players almost as much control over the adventure as the person who is running the game. For example, during an adventuring session, the GM may ask the players how they know a given non-player character (or NPC), giving each player a chance to "write" part of the story using their own imagination on the spot. Therefore if you are considering running a Dungeon World, you'll want to seek out a group of players who are very interested in collaborative storytelling or improvisational play.

⊚ Cthul-WHO? Horror Role-Playing Games for the Library

Aside from fantasy, the next popular genre of role-playing games is horror. Call of Cthulhu, based on the works of cosmic horror author H. P. Lovecraft, is the granddaddy of horror role-playing games, with even more rules editions than D&D—there was even a ruleset for Call of Cthulhu made with the open-gaming d20 license! Instead of delving into dungeons in search of monsters to slay and treasures to collect, in Call of Cthulhu the players are cast in the roles of various Investigators who must unravel various occult plots lest the forces of mighty Cthulhu and the other Old Ones be unleashed upon the mortal realm. While physical combat can be an important part of the game, Call of Cthulhu emphasizes using your wits and guile instead, rewarding characters for performing research (there's even a Library Use skill), gathering clues and evidence, and solving puzzles. Moreover, even if they succeed in saving the day, the Investigators are permanently affected by their adventures, as each player has a Sanity score, which is slowly but surely chipped away at by witnessing both the horrific and the supernatural. Once an Investigator reaches zero Sanity, their character is no longer playable and must be retired, but players may also experience shorter-term insanity during gameplay that they are required to roleplay. Sanity is also lost when occult knowledge is gained—for example, when a player reads a long-lost tome about the Cthulhu mythos—a grim gaming mechanic that fits the tone of H. P. Lovecraft's oeuvre perfectly.

Obviously Call of Cthulhu is not a role-playing game meant for everyone, but it is a frighteningly delightful alternative to Dungeons & Dragons, especially for players who are already familiar with the works of H. P. Lovecraft. However, if you are looking to play something scary without piling on the existential angst, you might want to consider some of the following options:

1. Chill (Growling Door Games, 2015). A horror RPG that made its debut in 1984 but was overshadowed by the more successful and recognizable Call of Cthulhu, Chill is a little more freewheeling and action-based, sending the players around the world as envoys of a secret organization known as S.A.V.E. to rid the world of evil creatures such as vampires, mummies, and werewolves.

2. Kult (Helmgast AB, 2016). Another classic of the horror RPG genre originally released in 1991, Kult is a Swedish role-playing game where the players are slowly introduced to the key concept that the real world is not what it seems to be and that mankind has been held captive by sinister forces that will stop at nothing to keep the world in ignorance. Equal parts Gnostic theology and cinematic horror set to rules that allow for a wide range of play, Kult has been likened to the role-playing equivalent of a Rorschach inkblot: the system and setting are surprisingly flexible so that the players can explore almost any aspect of the horror genre they wish, as broadly and/or deeply as they dare.

3. World of Darkness (White Wolf/Paradox). Once upon a time the role-playing game genre was taken by storm by a game called Vampire: The Masquerade. Published in 1991 by White Wolf, Vampire: The Masquerade introduced the RPG world to a new kind of narrative-heavy system where instead of playing vampire hunters, the players would play vampires instead, dealing not only with the normal conflicts inherent to any role-playing game but forcing each player to wrestle with their internal demons as they struggled to keep what remained of their humanity intact. The combination of emo storytelling with a neo-gothic setting created a perfect storm when the game first hit the market in 1991, enchanting a generation of RPG gamers who had been steadily losing interest in D&D over time. Vampire: The Masquerade was quickly supplemented by parallel rulebooks for role-playing as werewolves, sorcerers, and even mummies, all of which comprised what became known as the World

of Darkness (or WoD) RPG setting. After several iterations of the WoD setting, White Wolf Publishing was purchased by Paradox Interactive, which is promising a fifth edition of Vampire: The Masquerade. Given the original popularity of this franchise, the nostalgia factor alone may bring in a large percentage of former players along with people just discovering the game, just as D&D's fifth edition has, so this particular RPG might be worth revisiting in the not-so-distant future.

4. Dread (The Impossible Dream, 2005). Winner of the 2006 ENnie Award for Innovation, the horror RPG Dread eschews rolling dice by making players draw from a Jenga tower—yes, from the classic board game Jenga—whenever they want to perform an action during the session where the outcome may be in doubt. If the player can remove a block from the tower, the action succeeds; if the player refuses to pull a block from the tower, the action fails. If the player attempts to pull a block from the tower and knocks it over, however, their character is removed from the game, either by death or some horrifying alternative. Complex or difficult tasks may require more than one pull to be successful, per the GM's ruling. What makes this mechanic perfect for a horror scenario is that the Jenga tower becomes progressively more unstable as the game proceeds, mirroring and contributing to the rising tension levels in the adventure until at some point in the latter portion of the game, any action could very well end in tragedy. While Dread comes with its own ruleset including rules for character creation and several different settings, the simplicity of its mechanics means that it can be used with practically any combination of characters and setting that you wish. It is also a fun game to watch, which makes it particularly useful for a library gaming program.

5. Tales From The Loop (Simon Stålenhag and Fria Ligan AB, 2017). If a horror role-playing game that uses a Jenga tower to resolve actions and conflict isn't strange enough for you, then perhaps one based on a weird Swedish artbook might be more to your liking. Tales From The Loop puts the players in the role of kids growing up in a weird alternate version of the 1980s that never was, where Cold War science has brought us giant robots, hover cars, and other shiny automated things promised by the futurists of yesteryear. All is not right in this retro-futuristic utopia, however, with a series of weird events occurring that are related to the particle accelerator (hence the eponymous "Loop") that so happens to be in your hometown. Both the setting and the rules are meant to be viewed through the lens of childhood nostalgia, with adults being inherently untrustworthy—indeed, when a character turns sixteen, they are removed from play—and the character "Classes" being the high school stereotypes of Jock, Weirdo, Geek, and others. However, this includes elements of psychological horror as well, with characters being able to be broken not just by monsters and secret government agencies but by the things that haunt real adolescents and teenagers: divorce, abuse, bullying, and sexual confusion. Reviewers have called Tales From The Loop "*Stranger Things*: The Roleplaying Game"—given the current obsession with 1980s nostalgia, this horror RPG certainly resonates with the times in a way that others do not.

◎ Other Genres, Other Worlds

If neither fantasy nor horror are to your patrons' liking, do not despair—there are role-playing games available that correspond to almost every genre of entertainment.

While a complete rundown of the current RPG market would be well beyond the scope of this book, let us at least take a quick look at the following genres and their most popular offerings:

- post-apocalyptic
- Old West
- cyberpunk
- science fiction
- superheroes

ⓖ *Mad Max: Fury Road* with Funny Dice

The post-apocalyptic genre has been a staple of the RPG market since almost the very beginning, with TSR releasing its Gamma World setting in 1978, just a few years after it published the original Dungeons & Dragons ruleset. Instead of a world full of magic and monsters drawn heavily from faerie tales, world mythology, and the fantasy novel genre, Gamma World thrust its players into a future set centuries after World War III where radiation had mutated most plants and animals into strange and dangerous beasts and given human beings extraordinary powers. The characters roam the ruins of our own civilization in search of adventure, riches, and the lost technology of the Ancients, who were considered to be almost magical and godlike in their powers. Gamma World has enjoyed several editions over the years, with its most recent ruleset (Wizards of the Coast, 2010) being fully compatible with the fourth edition rules for Dungeons & Dragons.

While there have been rumors of a new edition of Gamma World to complement the latest edition of D&D, in the meantime there are several other RPGs available to scratch that post-apocalyptic itch, with varying levels of realism and grit. Apocalypse World (Lumpley Games, 2016) uses the same basic rules system as the collaborative fantasy RPG Dungeon World, relying heavily on the players to share in the world-building and storytelling aspects of role-playing. Mutant Future (Goblinoid Games, 2010) has more of a classic feel that hearkens back to the original version of Gamma World—moreover, it is compatible with Goblinoid Games' 2016 Apes Victorious, which is a sourcebook for running an authentic *Planet of the Apes*–style apocalypse! In a similar vein, Atomic Highway (Cubicle 7 Entertainment Ltd, 2010) is a "rules-light" system that evokes the setting of *Mad Max*, although when discussing the hyper-violent automotive subgenre of post-apocalyptic fiction, we would be remiss if we left out GURPS: Autoduel, which is an RPG system designed to supplement Car Wars, a battle-royale-style board game where players outfit their cars with weapons, armor, and other tricks to compete in the late twenty-first century's version of a demolition derby.

If your patrons are fans of the enormously popular post-apocalyptic computer RPG game Fallout, there are several RPGs that emulate the Fallout series in terms of theme and tone: The Morrow Project (TimeLine, 2013), now in its fourth edition, and Exodus (Glutton Creeper/4 Hour Games, 2008), which was originally published as an officially licensed Fallout RPG using the d20 Modern system before losing its license from Bethesda Softworks, who is in the process of releasing its own Fallout hybrid board game/tabletop RPG. The generic RPG systems GURPS and Savage Worlds also have their own sourcebooks for converting their rulesets to emulate Fallout as closely as possible, and if that were not enough, there is a twenty-eight-page self-contained system called Retrocalypse created by the retro RPG gaming community using something called the "Old School Hack," which applies a reductionist, old-school RPG rules treatment to the specific post-apocalyptic setting of the Fallout series (fictivefantasies.files.wordpress.com/2012/07/retrocalypse-8-18-11-final.pdf).

We will take a closer look at the active home-brew and "modding" communities in gaming in chapter 11, but at the moment it is interesting to point out the extent to which the RPG gaming community has embraced the DIY and Maker philosophies, be it consciously or unconsciously. There isn't an RPG community out there that hasn't issued its own set of house rules that supplement or supersede existing rulesets—from here it's not difficult to envision rewriting or "hacking" entire systems in order to improve or enhance gameplay for the group or just as a sideline experimental hobby/diversion. For example, I have a gamer friend who is always willing to mod or home-brew a new set of rules for several different kinds of tabletop RPGs, whether or not he has any intention of playing using said rules.

⑥ The Shattered Frontier, the Weird West, and the Dogs in the Vineyard: Wild West RPGs

Role-playing games set in the Wild West, while perhaps not as popular as the fantasy, horror, or post-apocalyptic RPG settings, nevertheless have a lineage stretching back to the early days of Dungeons & Dragons, with TSR's publication of Boot Hill in 1975. Unlike D&D, however, which grew out of its miniatures ruleset to embrace a world of fantastic creatures and imaginative magic systems, Boot Hill remained grounded in its origins first and foremost as a set of tactical rules instead of a fully developed role-playing game, and as such never gained the popularity that other early offerings from TSR did. It wasn't until later that the genre ended up with several viable options for players. Aces & Eights (Kenzerco, 2007) is a fairly straightforward system for playing one of myriad characters in the Old West, with rules covering how to drive cattle and prospect for gold, but it is set in an alternate history where the U.S. Civil War ended in a draw, with the competing states of the Republic of Texas, Deseret, and Sequoyah vying with the USA, CSA, and Imperial Mexico for control of the vast riches of the American West. Deadlands (Pinnacle, 2006), on the other hand, imagines an alliance of Native American shamans opening a portal to another dimension, which transforms the Old West into the "Weird West," a land of undead gunslingers, demon spirits, and other magical elements. For a less fantastic and more historical Wild West RPG experience, Sidewinder: Reloaded (Dog House Rules, 2004), based off the d20 Modern system, may be an older offering, but it offers a comprehensive ruleset for role-playing in the authentic Old West without resorting to any gimmicks such as combining genres or altering the area's history.

An unusual but noteworthy entry to the Old West RPG genre is Dogs in the Vineyard (Lumpley Games, 2004), voted Indie RPG of the Year and Most Innovative Game in 2004. In Dogs in the Vineyard, the players all take the role of "God's Watchdogs" in a fictionalized version of the Mormon State of Deseret in pre-statehood Utah. These watchdogs (or dogs) travel from town to town as representatives of the faith and are called upon to resolve disagreements, root out heresy, and perform other heroic tasks as needed. What makes Dogs in the Vineyard special is that it was the first RPG to introduce the concept of "Say yes or roll," a variation on the improv theater rule of thumb "Yes, and . . . ," which encourages participants to accept what another participant has already stated and then build upon that idea. With "Say yes or roll," a GM is agreeing to either allow players to participate in the storytelling process or roll to contest their efforts. While many RPGs now embrace this shared narrative approach to storytelling, when Dogs in the Vineyard first appeared in 2004, this was a relatively new concept, and one which bordered on heresy in some gaming design circles. Even though this "narrativist" flavor of gaming is firmly established in such systems as Apocalypse World/ Dungeon World, there is still a vocal minority of gamers who believe that the DM or GM's word should be law and the players should not have such a level of creative control over the game itself.

⊚ Role-Playing in the Matrix: Cyberpunk RPGs

William Gibson's 1984 novel *Neuromancer* helped mainstream the genre of cyberpunk, a dystopian brand of science fiction where mastery of information technology and cybernetics are the keys to prosperity in a world where corporations have subverted the social order and most of mankind now lives in a perpetual state of desperate squalor. Not surprisingly, the cyberpunk genre has proven to be a popular setting for many role-playing game systems, as it provides an almost inexhaustible source of potential adventures in a universe that is only limited by one's imagination. The first and most classic iteration of the cyberpunk genre is Cyberpunk 2020, also known as Cyberpunk 2013 or Cyberpunk 203X, originally released in 1988 by R. Talsorian Games. In this game, players adopt various roles in the fictitious dystopian future metropolis known as Night City, each with their own Special Ability—for example, Netrunners have the special ability to Interface with the Net, while Corporate characters have the ability to tap their employer's resources to help them in the adventure. Players can also augment themselves with cybernetics and other kinds of futuristic technology, including weapons, although combat is designed to be quick and lethal and problem-solving is encouraged instead. Although the third edition of Cyberpunk is already more than ten years old, as of the time of writing this book, a fourth edition—titled Cyberpunk 2077—is currently in development along with a video game RPG version by the same name, with an expected release date in early 2019.

Although Cyberpunk 2020 has the distinction of being the first cyberpunk game, the most popular RPG in the genre currently is Shadowrun, now in its fifth edition, which was published in 2013. Like Cyberpunk 2020, Shadowrun is set in a dystopian future dominated by greedy megacorporations, but unlike its predecessor, Shadowrun incorporates fantasy elements, with magic having erupted into the world following the end of the Mesoamerican Long Count in 2012 and the beginning of what the game calls the "Sixth World." Players find their work as shadowrunners, adventurers for hire who vie for contracts from corporate fixers in need of expendable subcontractors to do their dirty work, which can range from espionage to assassination; true to the genre, almost every job will involve one or many reversals of fortune or betrayals, as rival corporations attempt to beat the party to their objective with their own machinations (or even rival subcontracted shadowrunners!). Shadowrun has an enormous and loyal fanbase, as its mixture of fantasy and cyberpunk elements makes it appealing to both science fiction and fantasy gamers. As such, it makes for an interesting alternative to generic Dungeons & Dragons, so if your library has someone familiar with Shadowrun and willing to run it, you may want to consider it for your library gaming programming.

From Science Fiction to Space Opera: Sci-Fi RPGs

Although cyberpunk is definitely a subgenre of science fiction, it is popular enough to get its own treatment for the purposes of this book, but this does not mean that there aren't many science fiction RPGs to choose from. In fact, the granddaddy of all science fiction RPGs, Traveller, is also one of the oldest continuously running role-playing games, with its first edition published in 1977 by Game Designers' Workshop and its most current edition released in 2016 by Mongoose Publishing. Traveller is designed as an open-ended "sandbox" adventuring system where players have the freedom of doing almost anything they want—they can play as scouts and explore the galaxy, join the marines or the navy and go to war, lease a small spaceship and find their fortune as a merchant, or any of a variety of other roles. If Traveller is known for anything, however, it is for its character generation process, where each player determines their prior experience and skills in four-year increments called terms. For each term, the player decides what they would like to do, then rolls to see how well they fared doing said activity. If a player rolls poorly enough during this phase, they can either be forced out of their chosen profession or even die on the job! Traveller is also replete with tables and charts for randomly generating spaceships, planets, and entire solar systems, so make sure that this kind of game appeals to your audience before trying to launch a Traveller campaign in your library—there's a lot of math and a lot of die-rolling but also the joy of exploring a slowly unfolding, procedurally generated universe where literally anything could be waiting for you to discover just beyond the next star system.

If space opera is more your thing, then you may want to consider the *Star Wars* RPG instead. The original version of the game, published by West End Games between 1987 and 1996, was not just massively popular, but the sourcebooks and adventure supplements—all of which were licensed by Lucasfilm—were considered to be so authoritative until Disney's reboot of canon in 2014 that novelists writing in the *Star Wars* genre (such as Timothy Zahn, best-selling author of the Thrawn Trilogy) used them for reference! Just as kids playing with *Star Wars* toys helped stoke the popularity of the original trilogy in between film releases, the *Star Wars* RPG kept the franchise alive in the imaginations of a generation between *Return of the Jedi* and *The Phantom Menace*. Subsequent editions of the *Star Wars* RPG were released by Wizards of the Coast, who wed the *Star Wars* setting to its then-ubiquitous d20 ruleset, between 2000 and 2010 and thereafter by Fantasy Flight Games, who republished a completely redesigned set of rules and sourcebooks in 2012 featuring customized colored dice and an emphasis on collaborative storytelling.

Finally, there is a fresh entry into the science fiction RPG genre: Starfinder, published by Paizo Games in 2017. Set in the far future of the Pathfinder fantasy universe (see above under fantasy RPGs for more about Pathfinder), Starfinder blends science fiction with fantasy in the same way that Shadowrun combines fantasy and cyberpunk. The result is a unique setting with novel twists on both the standard sci-fi and fantasy tropes, with a ruleset that is similar enough to Pathfinder and Dungeons & Dragons that veteran players of these games will find it easy to pick up the new system. As Starfinder has only just been released at the time of writing this chapter, it is difficult to assess how popular this RPG will prove to be, but given its successful lineage and cross-genre appeal, it would be surprising if Paizo did not have another best-selling game on their hands.

The last major subgenre of role-playing games that I will examine here is that of superhero RPGs. Not surprisingly, there are many superhero role-playing games available to choose from, as who wouldn't want to pretend to be a comic book hero or villain? Perhaps the most enduring superhero RPG title is Mutants & Masterminds (Green Ronin Publishing, 2002). Based on—yes, you guessed it—the d20 system, Mutants & Masterminds takes the core OGL rules and heavily expands and reskins them to include the world of superpowers, with the result that the system hardly feels like the original underlying "fantasy" ruleset at all. What makes Mutants & Masterminds so beloved to the superhero RPG community, however, is its own willingness to let other game writers and designers piggyback on their own copyrighted material to publish their own compatible adventures and rules supplements. Known as the "Superlink Program," this brand sharing has fostered a rather robust ecosystem of third-party publications. Mutants & Masterminds is also sufficiently generic a system so as to permit GMs to set their campaigns in any of a number of licensed superhero settings, such as the Marvel or DC Comics universes; indeed, there are published supplements that introduce a multitude of heroic settings, both those based on existing comics and others that are original creations.

It's not often that the leading alternative to a popular role-playing game was designed by the same person who created the most popular title, but in the case of superhero RPGs, perhaps one should expect the unexpected. Icons (Green Ronin Publishing, 2014) was developed by Steve Kenson as a lighter, faster, and less math-intensive alternative to his original brainchild, Mutants & Masterminds. Indeed, Kenson describes Icons as a "pick-up game," where players unfamiliar with the system can sit down and have a playable hero character ready in fifteen minutes or less. Icons also simplifies task and conflict resolution down to the roll of two six-sided dice and further lessens the importance of rolling dice by introducing a pool of Determination Points that enable players to seize a certain amount of narrative control over the game for a cost: players can use Determination Points to change the focus of or ensure success on a task, use their superpowers in a new and unexpected fashion, recover from damage and fatigue quickly, or even perform a "retcon" and change a previously unknown part of the setting or adventure to the player's advantage. Depending on how much your players enjoy getting enmeshed in the nitty-gritty of character creation and having a specific rule govern whether or not their hero can or cannot do something, or whether they would prefer to worry less about the rules and the rolls and more about the story being told, there is a game system at each end of the superhero RPG spectrum waiting to be explored.

Another extremely popular superhero RPG is Champions, published by Hero Games (natch) first in 1981, with the sixth and most recent edition released in 2010. The Champions system is noteworthy in a couple of respects. It was one of the first RPGs to allow players to allocate points to "purchase" their base character abilities, skills, and powers rather than determine them randomly or semi-randomly using dice rolls and tables. Also, its rules governing superpowers allow for a significant amount of customization, with players choosing from a set of generic effects and personalizing them to make them fit their character thematically. Instead of character classes, Champions gives the players a list of archetypes from which to choose, each with its own benefits and hindrances—such as Brick, who is slower and tougher in combat; Gadgeteer, representing a hero whose powers stem from technological devices; or Patriot, a character who is regarded as the embodiment of their nation, like Captain America. Another interesting note about Champions is that it is now part of the larger Hero System, which applies the same ruleset to other genres, such as fantasy, pulp action, and science fiction.

Finally, we would be remiss in addressing the topic of superhero RPGs without at least mentioning game systems that were specifically licensed by one or the other major comic book conglomerates. While DC had its own DC Heroes system, published by Mayfair Games, it was relatively short-lived (1985–1993) and is currently out of print. Marvel Comics on the other hand has had several different superhero RPG iterations, but none more successful and beloved than the original rules—also known as the FA-SERIP system, based on each character's primary attributes (Fighting, Agility, Strength, Endurance, Reason, Intuition, and Psyche)—which TSR published in 1984 as a Basic sixteen-page ruleset and thereafter as an Advanced system in 1986. The heart of the Marvel FASERIP system is the Universal Results Table, a tricolor chart whereby any task or challenge can be resolved by rolling two ten-sided dice and reading them as a percentage (d100 or "percentile dice"), comparing the result against the Power Level of the character. Effects are characterized by White, Green, Yellow, and Red results, each of which corresponds to an ascending level of failure and success. Although the original Marvel rules system is out of print, tracking down a copy of the Basic or Advanced set on eBay or Amazon is not impossible; FASERIP, a stripped-down generic (i.e., non-Marvel branded) version of the ruleset is also available as a free download on most online RPG stores—such as DriveThruRPG.com.

Why go to all of this trouble to try and play a role-playing game that is out of print and long since defunct? In the words of Steve Kenson, creator of both Mutants & Masterminds and Icons, speaking of the Marvel Superheroes system: "It's a testament to the game's longevity that it still has enthusiastic fan support on the Internet and an active play community more than a decade after its last product was published. Even more so that it continues to set a standard by which new superhero roleplaying games are measured. Like modern comic book writers and artists following the greats of the Silver Age, modern RPG designers have a tough act to follow." Even if your players ultimately end up choosing a more recent superhero RPG, the Marvel/FASERIP game is worth at least some consideration.

How About a Nice Dungeons & Dragons Board Game Instead?

As if there weren't already enough entry points into the world of Dungeons & Dragons, Wizards of the Coast took advantage of the extremely tactical fourth edition ruleset to create a series of board games called the D&D Adventure System Series, which allow for players to experience the basics of fantasy role-playing—i.e., playable characters, exploration, monsters, treasures, and funny-looking dice—without the need for a Dungeon Master or additional preparation above and beyond the rules and components that come with the game. In other words, each board game is its own self-contained Dungeons & Dragons adventure! Moreover, each board game explores an iconic classic "dungeon module" or series of dungeon modules (such as horror classic Castle Ravenloft and the epic fantasy quest Temple of Elemental Evil; fans of R. A. Salvatore can play the Legend of Drizzt as none other than Drizzt Do'Urden, the famous antihero of Salvatore's best-selling D&D novels) so that these games can appeal not just to newbies interested in learning more about D&D but would be of interest to veteran role-players as well who may very well have played the original adventures at some point in their gaming.

In each of these games, the players will choose one of several hero characters: a rogue, warrior, cleric, wizard, or one of the other D&D classes. As the players explore the dungeon/setting, they will turn over new tiles on the board, which will in turn reveal monsters or other kinds of challenges. As these are cooperative board games, players have to work together in order to defeat the monsters and other challenges, gaining treasure and experience points as they do so. In these games the players are able to improve themselves as they amass enough experience points to "level up." Each board game comes with several missions, which allow characters to continue from mission to mission as they improve their abilities and skills after successfully completing a previous adventure—it is even possible to combine all of the components from the various board games in the series to create a larger and much more random "megadungeon" as well! The myriad plastic miniatures that come with each game are also a great opportunity for your patrons to paint, either as its own activity or part of a larger miniatures painting event (see chapter 11 for more information about painting miniatures).

Not Just for Teens and Nostalgic Adults: RPGs for Kids

While it is entirely possible that younger gamers may be emotionally prepared to play any of the aforementioned titles without the need for extensive therapy later on in life, the sheer amount of casual violence and occult references in most role-playing games makes them problematic for preteen or adolescent audiences, especially when you are sponsoring these games through the venue of your library. (This in itself is rather amusing, as on the whole RPGs are much less graphic or explicit than they used to be in the 1970s and 1980s—especially so D&D, which not only has toned down the gore but also eliminated references to demons and devils in the 1990s and has a list of proscribed topics that the modern sourcebooks may not endorse, such as slavery and drugs.) So what's a Dungeon Master to do if a bunch of kids show up at the table wanting to play? The simplest answer would be to run a separate D&D campaign just for the kids, with less emphasis on the rules and more focus on the storytelling aspect of role-playing, but not every Dungeon Master would feel comfortable modifying their game on the fly in this way. Also, even when modified in this regard, Dungeons & Dragons is fundamentally about slaying monsters and acquiring treasure, so unless the objectives of the game are also modified to suit a younger audience, you may still run into problems—either with the young players or their apprehensive parents.

Fortunately we've reached a critical point in the development of role-playing games that creating safe points of entry for the next generation of gamers is enough of a marketing niche to support an entire ecosystem of RPGs for kids—indeed, most of these products are the brainchild of veteran gamers wrestling with how to introduce their own kids to their hobby. We will take a brief tour of the most popular kids' RPGs currently on the market, with an attempt to cover several different genres for the sake of diversity, as well as include one Honorable Mention of my favorite family RPG, which is suitable for any/all ages.

- No Thank You, Evil. An ENnie Award–winning RPG from Monte Cook Games, No Thank You, Evil is written for kids aged five and up. The game is set on the

Island of Storia, a magical place like Narnia, which can be visited through the back of your closet or by going under your bed, where the players look for adventure by helping people in need. Characters are created with story prompts, such as "_____ is a _____ _____" (e.g., Tom is a Silly Swordsman), which determine their basic attributes and special abilities; action is resolved through collaborative storytelling, solving puzzles, and rolling dice. With its emphasis on imagination and creativity and rules that can be scaled in complexity to accommodate older and younger children alike, No Thank You, Evil is a fantastic introduction to the world of role-playing games for kids.

- Hero Kids. Another ENnie Award winner, Hero Kids is a fantasy RPG for kids aged from four to ten from Hero Forge Games. Although at first it appears to be just a simplified version of Dungeons & Dragons or Pathfinder, the conceit is clever: the players are the children of adult adventurers who leave their kids to protect the town of Rivenshore from danger while they head out on yet another epic quest to save the world. And apparently there are many dangers for the Hero Kids to deal with! Characters are pregenerated, but there are enough of them with a sufficient amount of unique traits for players to feel some sense of personalization when they choose them. Actions are resolved using a pool of six-sided dice and the mechanics are sufficiently streamlined so that combat is quick and easy. There are also several expansions and supplements to keep the adventures going in Rivenshore, with the option of adding more complicated rules for older players like in No Thank You, Evil! As such, Hero Kids is a great entry-level fantasy role-playing game.

- Little Wizards. Originally released in French in 2005 by Le Septième Cercle as Contes Ensorcelés, Little Wizards takes kids to the planet of Coinworld, a disc-shaped world with an ocean and endless archipelagos to be explored on one side and a darker, more sinister mirror image of the same on the other. Players get to be sorcerers and mages who roam this fantastic two-sided universe in search of adventure. The rules for Little Wizards are similar to that of other kids' RPGs but with some interesting differences: for example, characters in Little Wizards do not have traditional combat attributes such as armor class and hit points, and it is impossible for the players to "lose" the game by dying or failing at a critical task. In fact, learning that failure isn't always a bad thing is an important theme of Little Wizards, with the Narrator/GM encouraged to creatively spin disasters into victories instead. If you are looking for a fantasy RPG for kids that emphasizes storytelling over combat, Little Wizards might just be the perfect choice.

- Mouse Guard. Based on the Eisner-winning comic book of the same name, Mouse Guard (Archaia Studios, first edition 2008; second edition 2015) is technically not an RPG designed for kids, but the setting—anthropomorphic swashbuckling mice in an alternate middle ages populated by other sentient woodland creatures—is just enchanting enough to make it worth the stretch with preteens and teenaged gamers. The system itself is a thematic simplification of the popular but somewhat complicated Burning Wheel RPG, where players create their characters by defining their overriding belief, immediate goal, a guiding instinct, and various traits that help round out the process. Actions are resolved by rolling six-sided dice, with each action following the narrative principle of Let It Ride, whereby any success or failure will advance the story in some way, anticipated or not. Combat follows an innovative model: characters must plan our their actions three moves in advance, rock/paper/scissors style; similarly, the GM determines each session's plot by using a combination of threats (animals, mice, weather, and wilderness), two of which are known to the players and the other two held as plot twists to be revealed and sprung on the players during the course of the adventure. While it would require an experienced GM to run it, especially for a younger audience, Mouse Guard is a dramatic romp through a richly imagined universe and definitely worth the extra effort.

- Infestation. If there were a contest for the grossest of kids' RPGs, Infestation would almost certainly win the award. Published in 2014 by Third Eye Games, Infestation is a game where players take the role of intelligent bugs who struggle for survival in a filthy house overrun with even filthier humans, their mangy pets, and, of course, other bugs. Each player can choose from several different kinds of bug species, each with its own set of special abilities, diet, and favorite room in the house. The players work together to find food, scare humans, and defeat various threats to the house, including invaders like birds, lizards, and snakes. Tasks are resolved by rolling a series of white dice corresponding to the character's ability and other modifiers and black dice corresponding to the difficulty of the task—a die reading four or greater counts as a success, with white and black successes canceling each other out. If there are more white successes, the task succeeds; if there are more black, the tasks fails; in the case of a tie, the task barely succeeds. Easy to learn and fun to play, Infestation is a great game for kids who are into all things creepy-crawly.

- *Ghostbusters* the RPG. Just as we did for the Superhero RPG genre, we will end this section of kid-friendly role-playing games by recommending a system that is out of print but more than worth the trouble in acquiring: *Ghostbusters* the RPG, published in 1986 by West End Games. Based on the 1984 cult classic movie, the *Ghostbusters* RPG allows players to assume the role of paranormal investigators who launch their very own ghostbusting franchise. The rules are extremely simple, with an emphasis on action and storytelling—players can use Brownie Points to either re-roll their own dice or change the outcome of adverse effects. In this RPG version, the world of *Ghostbusters* is expanded to include not just ghosts and demigods but other supernatural entities such as vampires, werewolves, aliens, and even time travelers. With *Ghostbusters* as a perennial favorite and especially with the renewed interest in the *Ghostbusters* franchise with the 2016 reboot, this is a great choice for an RPG that is kid-friendly. After all, who doesn't want to be a Ghostbuster?

Ⓖ Key Points

- Role-playing games are enjoying an unprecedented surge in popularity due to wider acceptance in mainstream culture and a wave of 1980s nostalgia.
- Role-playing games are quintessential library-friendly forms of gaming—usually requiring several books as well as additional reading for research and inspiration.
- As with board games, libraries can serve as safe points of introduction to the RPG gaming hobby, providing spaces that are more welcoming to potentially marginalized gamers.

- Not only are there now five editions of Dungeons & Dragons to choose from, but there is an almost infinite variety of other RPGs set in other genres—just as libraries can feature new and unusual board games, they could feature less well-known RPGs at events as well.
- Role-playing games can have a huge MakerSpace component to them, printing out miniatures and terrain, crafting props and costumes, and so on.
- There are many age-appropriate RPGs for younger players, including games specifically designed for children under the age of ten and preteens.

How to Run a Library Trivia Event

IN THIS CHAPTER

▷ The Next Big Thing from the UK

▷ Getting Started, or Securing Buy-In from Stakeholders

▷ Choosing Your Venue

▷ Scheduling Your Pub Quiz: What Day of the Week Isn't the New Friday?

▷ Them's the Rules: Formatting Your Pub Quiz Event

▷ "Let's Get Quizzical!": A Sample Format

▷ Trivial Pursuits, or How to Craft Your Questions

▷ Planning to Plan, or the Importance of Overplanning

▷ For Your Eyes Only, or Keeping Your Trivia Questions Secret

▷ How to Draft the Perfect List of Trivia Question in Just Five Steps

▷ "It's Showtime!": Promoting/Hosting/Staffing Your Event

▷ Running the Show: Setting Up at Your Venue

▷ Evaluation and Assessment

▷ The Questions Are Too Hard!/The Hard Questions Are Why We Prefer Your Trivia!

▷ Incorporating Different Kinds of Challenges

▷ Sponsors and Other Special Events

▷ Conclusion: Community Outreach Made Fun

THE PUB QUIZ, ALSO KNOWN AS quiz night or trivia night, is a phenomenon that started in local pubs in the United Kingdom in the 1970s. The original impetus of the pub quiz was, not surprisingly, to draw in customers to come and drink on quieter nights of the week, but somewhere along the way it took on a life all its own. Since its inception in the 1970s, the pub quiz has become an established institution in British culture, with more than twenty-two thousand weekly quizzes taking place in 2009 and larger events held on regional and national levels as well. In the meantime, the pub quiz has found fertile ground here in the United States as well, with several thousand regular quizzes taking place each week and more and more places adopting the format—not just bars but also restaurants and other venues, with libraries getting into the game in recent years as well, either partnering with a local pub or hosting the event in their own space.

While there are now companies in the United States that will actually manage a pub quiz or trivia event (from this point forward in the chapter we will use these two terms interchangeably) for you from start to finish—for a modest fee, of course—creating and hosting your own pub quiz is not only well within your library's skill set, but it is a great form of community outreach as well. Running a trivia event where the questions have all been crafted by library staff lends a certain level of challenge to the event and puts a definite library spin on an event that could otherwise come off as being too slick, with a generic or corporate feel to it. Indeed, some libraries have adopted the trivia night as a fund-raising tool, using a per person cover charge to raise money for the library or other specific charities.

In this chapter we will show you how to run your own pub quiz/trivia event, examining in turn each of the following critical considerations:

1. getting started, or securing buy-in from stakeholders
2. choosing your venue
3. deciding upon the quiz night format
4. how to craft all of those wonderful questions
5. hosting/staffing the event (including promotion)
6. evaluation and assessment

Please note that although we will use the term pub trivia and that some of our examples will be drawn from library events being held at pubs, bar, or restaurants (for example, at the Westport Library our very successful series of Library Trivia Nights was held at a local bar and restaurant called 323 Main Street), it is by no means necessary to find an external host for your trivia night event. Although some communities are pleasantly surprised and happy to find their libraries partnering with local watering holes and eateries, it is understood that not all patrons groups may feel the same way about this, especially where events serving alcohol are concerned. What follows is a recipe for an event guaranteed to be fun for both patrons and staff, no matter what the venue!

⊚ Getting Started, or Securing Buy-In from Stakeholders

First things first. While these kinds of events can be great fun, running a trivia night represents a significant commitment of time, energy, and enthusiasm from your staff.

Not only is this true of getting the first event up and running, but trivia nights require a certain amount of recurring responsibility—such as coming up with new trivia questions for each event—if you intend to make this event a regular event in your library's programming calendar. Be sure that your staff are aware of what they are committing to, and that your managers and administrators understand what will be required of your staff as well, especially on the nights when you are actually hosting and running the event! Will you need additional resources to make this kind of event happen? For example, does the venue have their own audio-visual setup, or will you have to provide one? Will you have enough staff on hand for the event, or will you have to include more part-time staff or subs in order to make sure everything runs smoothly (and don't forget staffing your service desks back at the library!)? Are you pitching this as a onetime event, a seasonal series, or an ongoing weekly/biweekly/monthly kind of program? These are questions you will be expected to be able to answer before you are able to proceed with the next steps in the process of getting started.

Be realistic with yourself, your staff, and your stakeholders, but at the same time don't be afraid to say you're uncertain about a specific aspect of the event at this time. Although you can plan for many possible contingencies, it is almost inevitable that you will find a way to fail that you had not anticipated in advance (this is of course doubly true when dealing with any live public event). Do not let this rattle you, but try to get yourself in the mindset to expect the unexpected and your staff will hopefully follow suit. Nine times out of ten your audience won't even realize that something has gone wrong—and even in that tenth instance, remember that they are coming to your programming as supporters of the library and want you to succeed as much as you do. Have a good sense of humor about any potential adversity, and your patrons will more than forgive you for having the temerity to run a program that is less than perfect.

Choosing Your Venue

We have already mentioned earlier in this chapter that "pub quizzes" or "pub trivia" need not happen in an actual pub or bar but can be held in almost any kind of venue, including your own library. The question of whether to look for an external host is entirely up to you and what kind of audience you are seeking for this kind of event. As trivia nights have become an established feature of bars here in America just as they have in the United Kingdom, there is a certain guaranteed "captive audience" for these kinds of events if you can find the right partner to host. This is especially true if your area has a Pub Trivia Meetup group and you can become a regular stop along their list of favorite recurring events (more about Meetup and promotion below). On the other hand, holding it at a library or neutral event space such as a community center or function hall broadens the range of people able to attend the event to include younger and older demographics, as well as families who may have felt uncomfortable at the prospect of bringing their children to a pub.

No matter what location you choose for your trivia night event, you should be evaluating it along the following guidelines:

1. Space. Does the venue have enough seating to accommodate everyone attending the event? If your trivia night is standing room only, you probably want to find bigger digs for your event. Conversely, if the space is too big, you may lose a sense of intimacy and friendly competition among rival teams. There is a sweet spot here

for certain, a Goldilocks range of not too crowded but not too empty—hopefully as you host and run these events you'll get a feel for it.

2. Privacy. Do you have an entire space dedicated to your event so that participants won't have to struggle to keep up with what's going on? This can be the primary difficulty with hosting your trivia night at a bar—on less crowded nights, the regular drinkers can easily prove to be twice as stubborn and may not welcome a trivia group setting up shop in the middle of their local watering hole. Is there a way to subdivide existing space, or are there adjacent rooms (such as overflow dining rooms) you can use that may keep everyone happy and not in each other's faces? Remember—while the goal here is to achieve some extra visibility and outreach, you don't want to achieve either of these at the expense of your community's goodwill. Conversely, if you wish to hold this event at your own library, be mindful that even without the alcohol, pub trivia can be a loud and lively event, so be sure to earmark a large meeting room or schedule your trivia night as an after-hours event so that you can take over your library's ear- and airspace without protest.

3. Audio-visual concerns. It is very difficult to run a successful trivia night without using some kind of audio setup, as it is hard even with a microphone and amplification to cut over the ambient noise of a busy restaurant or bar. Although many external venues may have some kind of sound wiring on site, bear in mind that most touring musical acts bring their own audio equipment with them—and you should as well. Take this advice from a librarian who has gathered enough anecdotal evidence over the years: a modest investment in your own microphone and amplifier can save you from a world of headaches and last-minute panic attacks that happen when you encounter technical difficulties during a library program. The visual setup is more negotiable, however. The default format for one round of a pub quiz is to read each question aloud once or twice, then to display all of the questions for the round on a visual display that all of the teams can see for reference. However, if the venue does not have a suitable display, instead of bringing your own, you can opt to print out the questions for each round onto a set of team reference cards and hand these out after all of the round's questions have been read aloud (more about the pub quiz format below).

4. Partnership. A good pub quiz venue is not just someone who is going to let you use their space, but someone who sees the potential value in such an event not just for the library, but their own business and the community at large as well and partners with you accordingly to make sure that you are all doing the best possible job to plan, publicize, host, and run this kind of event. For example, does your host promote the event using their own mailing lists and PR distribution channels? Do they offer specials on drinks or food for pub quiz nights? Do they offer any prizes as well, such as discounts on the winning team's bar tab or a gift certificates for future visits? Having a partner who is just as invested in the success of the event as you are can make all of the difference.

⌖ Scheduling Your Pub Quiz: What Day of the Week Isn't the New Friday?

Finding the right time and day for your pub quiz event is equal parts voodoo and science. On the one hand, you want to try to pick as consistent a date as possible (e.g., the first

Thursday of every month); but on the other hand, real life intrudes and you can find yourself accidentally counterprogramming your own library's activities if you are too inflexible. Sometimes your venue will be able to suggest a good lull in their schedule when a boost in sales would be most beneficial to them. Just remember to make sure that you are coordinating with the stakeholders responsible for programming at your own library, as many of those slow evenings for bars and restaurants happen to be perfect scheduling slots for visiting authors or other special library events. If you have a good working relationship with your programming staff, ideally you can block your dates out as far in advance as possible so as to minimize the chance of any internal conflict. Keeping an eye on local sports and politics is probably a good idea as well, as trivia night does not fare well against a potentially fractured audience.

Also pay close attention to any other trivia events being held in your community. Try to schedule around these events, if at all possible. While there's nothing wrong with a little bit of healthy competition, there are also only so many would-be trivia enthusiasts to go around. Indeed, if you join a local trivia group on Meetup, you will find that it is generally speaking the same cohort that travels from venue to venue. The key to winning their attendance therefore is not to compete with any established events already in their schedule rotation but to find an opening and make it an opportunity to launch a brand new pub quiz event for their group to incorporate as one of their scheduled stops. As we have already seen in previous chapters, Meetup can be a powerful tool for finding not just trivia groups but virtually any special interest community you might want to reach out to for programming purposes.

The timing of the event is also important. If you start your pub quiz too early, you run the risk of stranding would-be players in traffic as they try to get from work to your venue. Start too late, however, and you may lose your ability to muster enough library staff to properly run the event from start to finish—also, bear in mind that bar crowds tend to get progressively louder and rowdier as the evening proceeds and that, grateful though they may be for the extra business, a restaurant may want to start closing up past a certain hour. Whatever you decide, it is very important that barring any serious weather or traffic concerns (like an accident on the highway or construction), you do your utmost to start and finish your trivia night as close to the advertised times as possible. The last thing you want to do is punish the people who came on time to your event—if this means starting with a couple of players or teams short, then so be it!

Finally, we should discuss how often you should run an event like this. Although many other venues that host trivia nights can do so on a weekly basis, it is important to remember that most of these places outsource the event to a third party that specializes in hosting trivia events, leveraging an economy of scale to ensure that they can deliver a consistent entertainment product week after week, whereas the library is relying on its own resources in order to pull off each and every pub quiz event. For all practical purposes, this probably puts a weekly trivia night beyond the capacity of even the most dedicated and motivated library staff—it is for this reason that I recommend a library commit to no more than one or two such events per month, especially when starting out. Tempting though it may be to do this kind of program as often as possible (and be warned that a venue may try to help you overcommit in this regard if you let them), your first responsibility is to make sure that the library can successfully execute the event from start to finish without putting any undue strain on library staff, resources, or morale. Events like pub trivia are meant to be fun, so the last thing you want to do is make running them feel like a chore. In the best case scenario, your staff should enjoy planning the event almost as much as they enjoy running it.

The international success of the pub quiz as a form of entertainment has resulted in there being myriad different ways for running trivia events. In this section, I will provide a quick overview of the most popular rules format and highlight a couple of variations that you may or may not want to implement. That being said, no matter what rules or format you decide upon, it is important to keep the following few guiding principles in mind:

1. The format should be fair. What does fairness mean here? The goal of trivia night should be for all players to have an enjoyable time, win or lose. For example, although reference librarians can pride themselves on coming up with the most diabolically obscure pieces of trivia, these do not necessarily make for the best questions at a pub quiz. People don't come to trivia night to feel stupid, but there are clever ways to challenge your audience nevertheless—we will discuss how to do this in the next section of this chapter. Another and perhaps more important example is having rules governing whether other library staff, volunteers, or stakeholders can play or not. Surely encouraging staff to turn out on trivia night is an important part of building buzz around the event, but if those same staff members end up winning the grand prize for the evening, you can inadvertently sour your non-library attendees on whether the game was in fact fair. A nice compromise for this situation is to allow staff to play if they weren't involved in writing the questions, but to make their team ineligible for any prizes, so that if they won first place, the second place team would win that prize instead.

2. The format should be transparent. Most reasonable people don't mind losing, as long as they feel like they've lost fair and square. This is why it is incumbent upon you and your staff to have a clear and consistent format for your pub quiz, including a full set of rules that you should go over with the players at the start of each session. Being transparent up front and throughout the entire event helps ensure that, even when players do have a gripe or bone to pick, they can rest assured that at the very least you are behaving as a fair and neutral party in resolving any disputes that may arise.

3. The format should evolve but only in between sessions. This may sound somewhat contradictory, but once you have endeavored to make sure that the format and rules are fair and that you have successfully communicated them to your contestants, you should try your hardest to stick to these rules for the evening. Hand in hand with this should be an advisory to the effect that any ruling that the staff or other designated judges make should be considered final for the event. The only thing worse than getting bogged down in the minutiae of a rules interpretation is making a ruling and then changing it. Remember that your attendees expect fair play first and foremost—demonstrating that you are applying the rules as written or communicated consistently throughout the library trivia event is your best possible defense against any accusations to the contrary.

That being said, you should definitely be willing to learn and adapt as you go. We will explore proper evaluation and assessment for an event like pub trivia at the conclusion of this chapter, but in the meantime try to schedule at least one informal debrief with your participating staff after every event. It can be just a stand-up meeting the morning afterward or even over drinks at the bar following the conclusion of pub quiz, but be sure to have the meeting/discussion as soon as possible after you finish so that everyone's impressions of what worked during the event and what didn't are still fresh in their minds.

⑥ "Let's Get Quizzical!": A Sample Format

The following basic pub quiz format is a generic version of the one adopted by the reference and experiential learning staff at the Westport Library in Westport, Connecticut, for our monthly trivia night at a local bar and restaurant. Each section of the rules will include some commentary about why we chose what we chose and how you may want to implement something different.

1. Teams shall consist of up to four players.

To be honest, enforcing team size was always the most difficult thing we had to do. While most of the trivia-goers came in groups of four or less, there were a couple of larger groups who insisted on playing together. While we don't think it provided any real benefit to the team (in fact, one of the teams claimed that they wanted to sit together because none of them were any good at trivia), it was hard to shake the other players' perception that it would be an advantage, so we found ourselves constantly trying to strike a balance between fair play and everyone having a good time. From the latter viewpoint, we think we did the right thing by not being sticklers about group size, but we were actively tinkering with mechanics to try and make forming larger teams less palatable—such as a penalty for groups of six or more, ineligibility for prizes (similar to library staff), or something else along those lines.

2. There will be four rounds of trivia, plus one wager round.

Our goal was to have our event run as close to two hours as possible, as that seemed like the ideal amount of time that patrons having dinner and drinks would be interested in lingering in order to play trivia. That worked out to roughly four full rounds of play for us. The wager round was part of a series of rules format experiments we were playing with, including double-points rounds, in order to keep the game fun for the teams that were being left behind by the front runners. (And yes, you will always have front runners—ours was from our county's Trivia Meetup group; a couple of times we had all-librarian teams from other public libraries as well whom we'd challenged in the spirit of friendly competition.) The wager round allowed each team to bet any, all, or none of the points they had acquired in the previous rounds on one question. To be fair, we informed the players of the category of the wager round question, but to keep things somewhat suspenseful, we asked that the teams commit to their bets before they heard the actual question itself. One popular variant we didn't implement but may be of interest to other pub quiz groups was the concept of the "Joker Round": upon hearing the topic or theme of the upcoming trivia round, each team was allowed to declare one of the rounds their Joker Round, which meant that all of the point values for that round would be doubled. This combines an element of strategy to each team's gameplay, as the Joker Round could either be chosen too early or too late in the game.

3. Each round will consist of ten trivia questions, except for the wager round, which will consist of one question. Our co-hosts will read each question twice, then give every team the printed list of questions for that round.

See above for a discussion of what your venue may or may not be capable of. If your venue has an easily accessed video screen that all of the teams can see, you may want to put the questions up on the board after they have been read. That being said, it is still important to read each question twice, as it's amazing what you will not be able to hear over a room of people having a good time.

4. Teams will have three songs to answer all ten questions (one song for the wager round).

For each round we would play three pop music songs while the teams worked. This was almost definitely overkill on our part, as most teams would have handed in their answer sheets by the end of the first song, and having too long a break in between rounds where nothing seems to be happening can drain the enthusiasm in a crowd fairly quickly. Also, enforcing a shorter time limit probably would have helped keep everyone on their toes and encouraged a more level playing field.

5. Our co-hosts will read the correct answers while the team answer sheets are graded and scores are tabulated.

We had one dedicated grader and tabulator for our trivia nights, who had just enough time to grade between four and ten teams per round. If you are expecting more players, you may want to consider a second or third grader to assist.

6. NO CHEATING! This means no looking up answers on your smartphones, no spying on other teams, and no bribing your co-hosts for the correct answers. Also, no asking a librarian either. "If it feels like cheating, it's probably cheating."

Our contestants seemed to enjoy a little bit of humor when we read our rules at the start of each trivia night; your mileage may vary. Practically speaking, trying to keep people from cheating is a nigh-impossibility, as you and your staff will probably be extremely busy already just making sure everything is running as planned. Hopefully your teams will do their best to abide by the honor system. During our inaugural year of pub trivia at the Westport Library, we did not catch anyone who was actually trying to cheat, so we hope that you encounter similar success in this regard.

7. All answers are final, all scores are final—no partial or extra credit. Also, there is no arguing with or swearing at your co-hosts, no fisticuffs, and most importantly there is no crying in Library Pub Trivia (except for tears of joy or tears of laughter).

We spoke earlier in this chapter about the fundamental importance of ensuring fair play through transparency and consistent application of the rules. Part of this is also reminding players that they are expected to give their hosts the benefit of the doubt that they are behaving in a transparent and consistent fashion.

8. Westport Library staff members are allowed to compete, but they are ineligible to win any prizes. If a team with a Westport Library staff member should win, the prize would go to the next eligible team with the highest points total. Everyone is eligible for bragging rights, however.

Again we had mentioned this earlier on. Getting other library staff members and stake-holders excited about trivia night is a critical component in building a level of buzz around the event, so you certainly don't want to tell these people that they can't play if they show up because playing is more than half of the fun. Our rule of thumb was that if you had nothing to do with the production of the trivia questions, you were allowed to compete—if you had worked on the questions, however, you were encouraged to join us to help out with logistics: handing out question and answer sheets, collecting forms, and so on.

> TIE BREAKER RULES: In the event of a tie after four regular rounds plus the bonus round, the winner of Library Pub Trivia night will be determined by one SUDDEN DEATH OVERTIME trivia question. For Sudden Death Overtime, each team will be represented by one player chosen by their teammates. The tie-breaker question will be asked and the first player to answer correctly will break the tie and win.

Our Tie Breaker Rules are a great example of the importance of anticipating possible outcomes and making sure you are prepared for them procedurally. The original rules did not include any provision for tie-breakers, so the first time we actually encountered a tie (our second month, if memory serves), we were caught flat-footed about how to resolve the impasse. Although our players were all forgiving and understanding that this was an unusual situation, being forced to scramble at the last minute was not pleasant for our staff, and we immediately came up with a draft set of tie-breaking rules afterward so as to avoid any potential future embarrassment along similar lines.

BONUS POINTS

- Show us your library card: (one point per team, onetime bonus).

We rather enjoyed coming up with little ways that each team could enhance their scores. The library card bonus is pretty standard for a library-sponsored pub quiz, but since the odds of every team having at least one person at the table who had a library card on them were almost always 100 percent, it felt like we could have been making this challenge more interesting. For example, maybe use the total amount of library cards in a team's possession as the final tie-breaker? Or let teams get the library card bonus for more than one round, provided that nobody uses their library card more than once? What we didn't think of at the time is that we could have flipped this on its head and made our trivia night event an opportunity to sign people up for library cards if they didn't have one.

- Be the first to hand in your answer card (one point per round, regular rounds only).

This was one of those tweaks that only looks like genius in retrospect. At first we intro-duced this rule in order to keep people from hanging on to their answer cards for the entire three songs in between rounds (which most of our teams were doing), but it had the unintended consequence of creating a race among teams to see who could turn their card in first. Sometimes this race was literally a footrace, with players stumbling over tables and chairs to turn their answer card in before anyone else could! This added layer of drama at the end of each round became fun to watch in and of itself, while at the same time shaved off the average amount of time needed between rounds as well.

- Get ALL of the answers right in a round (two points, regular rounds only).

We liked having this rule in place in conjunction with the bonus point for being first because it introduced a fundamental strategic tension into gameplay. Is it more important to be first and get that extra point, or do we want to take our time and try for a perfect score instead? Over a year of pub trivia, we only had one or two instances where a team got the points for both being first and getting a perfect score, so this risk/reward choice mechanic really does work.

- Come up with the most entertaining WRONG answer (one point per round and judges' discretion, regular rounds only).

This was also conceived as a fun way to keep teams who were not winning engaged in the game, and it quickly became one of our favorite parts of each round.

Certainly there are other kinds of bonus point rules variants available. One that again introduces the element of strategic play is the concept of including a "Jackpot"-style bonus question for each round of play. In the first round, this bonus would be worth two points; with each passing round, however, its point value would increase by two, so that the second-round bonus would be four, the third-round bonus six, and the fourth 8. With each round, the difficulty of the Jackpot bonus question would increase as well. The twist to the Jackpot question is that each team may only attempt to answer the question once—for example, if the team tries to answer the Jackpot bonus in Round 1, whether they get the answer right or not, they will not be able to try for the bonus in Rounds 2, 3, or 4. This becomes another calculation of risk vs. reward, with teams having to decide whether or not to take easy money or hold out for what might be a game-changing bonus . . . if they know the answer to the question, that is!

OUR FABULOUS PRIZES:

1. First Place: 50 percent off your team's tab
2. Second Place: 25 percent off your team's tab
3. Third Place: Forgiveness of Library Fines (Westport Library only) or your choice from the Basket of ARCs

Again, this is definitely something you'll want to work on with your venue. If you are hosting your trivia night event at the library, clearly you'll have to come up with some different prizes (although never underestimate the power of Advance Reader Copies!). We were fortunate in that our hosts were willing to extend the 50 percent and 25 percent discounts to our first- and second-place winners, but you could perhaps ask them for gift certificates if they won't take anything off anyone's tab. The forgiveness of library fines is always a funny prize to offer, although in a solid year of gameplay, we've never had anyone actually take us up on this. If you have a library café, maybe consider offering gift certificates there or perhaps a discount coupon for your used-book bookstore or gift shop if you have either/both of those. Vouchers for library experiences also make great prizes—for example, an hour using the HTC Vive or Oculus Rift or a free "go to the head of the line" ticket for popular library programming events. The possibilities are truly unlimited here, so by all means feel free to use your imagination.

⊚ Trivial Pursuits, or How to Craft Your Questions

The most important thing to mention here is that you are by no means obligated to create all of your pub quiz trivia questions from scratch. There are myriad trivia resources out there—both online and in print—that can help you get started, so feel free to use any of these as needed. Another great source for pub trivia questions are librarians who have run similar programs, as they are usually more than willing to share lists of their old questions and answers with colleagues who don't have as much time on their hands to write their own. Librarians are proud of their achievements, so don't be afraid to reach out and ask how they managed to accomplish them. Not only could you end up with sample questions that you could use for your own trivia night, but you can also pick their brains for best practices and their hard-won wisdom on what to avoid when launching your own pub quiz program.

All of this having been said, however, there's nothing quite like writing your own trivia questions. Not only do you have more control over the subject matter you'd like to quiz your contestants about, but by the same token you also have the flexibility to respond to your community's interests and level of expertise, which means you can spend less time looking for new questions and more time crafting and fine-tuning your trivia questions to suit your particular audience. If all goes well, not only do your library staff feel empowered for having come up with an evening of entertainment for your patrons, but the people who come to the pub quiz event walk away with a palpable sense of appreciation for the depth and breadth of your librarians' subject knowledge.

⊚ Planning to Plan, or the Importance of Overplanning

Committing to a regular trivia event means that you should treat coming up with each event's questions as a part of your library staff's workflow, no more or less legitimate than any other recurring responsibility they may have on their plates. As a manager, this means making sure your staff have enough time to work on this assignment both individually and as a group and to help reinforce whatever planning process you and your staff decide upon for brainstorming, writing, vetting, and proofreading each set of trivia questions. Ideally the planning process for each event's questions should begin as soon as the last pub trivia event is concluded. Not only does this capitalize on the momentum of your (hopefully) still-energized staff, but it also allows them to start brainstorming with the strengths and weaknesses of the last outing still firmly in everyone's mind so that this wisdom can help inform and guide the process. For the other goalpost, you should expect your library staff to be rehearsing and polishing the final draft set of questions no later than the week before the next pub trivia event.

How you expect and/or enable your staff to work together on a collective enterprise such as this often depends on how your library traditionally approaches collaborative work. Does your group prefer formal meetings, informal check-ins, or virtual work using a shared platform such as Dropbox, Google Docs, or Sharepoint? While it is not within the scope of this chapter to explore these various methods of collaboration, for the sake of example, we will assume that our hypothetical library is using Google Docs in order to share the list of trivia questions as it evolves from ideation to completion (in fact, Google Docs was how the reference staff collaborated on our monthly trivia question lists at the Westport Library).

🌀 For Your Eyes Only, or Keeping Your Trivia Questions Secret

In the interest of cultivating an aura of professionalism and ensuring the goal of fair play, the first thing you want to do is define your inner circle of library staff (and/or volunteers, if applicable) who will be assisting in some capacity with the creation of the list of pub trivia questions. These staff should be aware of the fact that what they are working on is not meant to be shared and that, by virtue of helping with this phase of preparations, they are ineligible for actually playing as a member of a pub quiz trivia team. While people might want to be involved, some of your library staff might genuinely want to support the event simply by turning up and playing, so it's important at this stage of the planning process to quickly and clearly define who is in and who is out of this inner circle.

At the Westport Library, we decided that all reference staff members—full-time, part-time, and even our interns—were part of the inner circle, so that whenever they were on duty and found themselves with a lull at the desk, they could open up the Google Doc with the list of questions in progress and jump in and contribute as time permitted (we also made sure that our full-time staff blocked out off-desk time specifically for working on these trivia questions). Although this meant that our reference staff was ineligible to play on trivia night, most of our staff were more than happy to come anyway and assist with the logistics of running the event; however, this meant that any library staff who weren't part of the reference department could come and compete along with other members of the library community.

However you define your inner circle of staff who are handling the trivia questions, be sure that you don't inadvertently break that circle by doing things like talking about question ideas in common space used by other staff or accidentally printing out a list of questions on a shared printer and forgetting to pick it up. Although we're not exactly dealing with nuclear secrets, any precaution you take here will help reinforce the sense among your staff that they are expected to keep this process a secret so as to maximize everyone's entertainment on the day/night of the pub trivia event.

🌀 How to Draft the Perfect List of Trivia Questions in Just Five Steps

Trivia questions may look deceptively easy to write, but once you actually see how much effort goes into crafting even a simple sample question, you will never feel the same way again about it. The most important thing here is the process itself. While it's entirely possible to crank out a bunch of questions without any additional editing, vetting, or polishing, this kind of rough workmanship will inevitably reveal itself, especially when you run into questions that don't sound nearly as clear to your audience as you thought they did in your head. Even if you ultimately streamline this process to your own institutional needs and your available local resources, please try to have some kind of multi-step editing process in place so that you catch the most egregiously offending questions if nothing else!

An ideal editing process would consist of five steps:

1. brainstorming
2. first edit
3. vetting
4. second edit
5. final polish

For the brainstorming phase, getting as many raw ideas out of your staff's heads and onto paper (or its virtual equivalent) is key. At this point the questions don't even have to be questions but even just ideas about potential questions that another more knowledgeable staff member may be able to fill out. As the questions assume some semblance of order, they pass into the first edit phase of the process, where each question is reviewed for the relevance of the content and the potential difficulty of the answer. Does this particular round of questions have an overarching theme? If so, now is the time to decide whether a given question fits into that theme or not. Questions that do not fit into the round's thematic scope can be saved and redeployed in a subsequent round or saved for a future list of trivia questions instead.

During the vetting stage of the process, your library staff will fact-check the answers to each trivia question, making sure that the answer is not only correct but isn't an ambiguous answer as well. Trivia Nights work best when you ask questions that can be answered in the simplest of formats: true or false, multiple choice, or an answer that responds to the question in a 1:1 correspondence. Otherwise, confusion may result with your players, and your staff may be asked to adjudicate complex or ambiguous answers on the spot on the occasion of the event (which, speaking from personal experience, is not fun, especially when there are points and potential prizes on the line!). A good vetting process removes the obvious errors and ensures a practical homogeneity of trivia questions to maximize the chances of everything proceeding smoothly on the night of the event.

This leads to the second edit, when the vetted questions are assembled into a final draft list, and the final polish, when each question is read aloud in a full walkthrough. You'd be surprised at how many questions can make it to the final polish only to end up sounding ambiguously or awkwardly phrased when the staff actually try to read it—or, as actor Harrison Ford supposedly said to *Star Wars* filmmaker George Lucas: "You can write this [censored], but you sure can't say it." Never underestimate the importance of reading each and every question out loud with your staff before doing so in front of a live audience.

"It's Showtime!": Promoting/Hosting/Staffing Your Event

Once you have established when and where you will be having your trivia night, finalized your rules and regulations, and polished your questions for the upcoming round, it's finally time to get this show started! I'm going to assume for the sake of showing a complete event cycle that you have chosen to host your pub quiz trivia night on a monthly basis and furthermore that you've chosen an externally hosted event and not something that you are hosting on-site at your own library. Even if neither of these are the case you should have very little difficulty adapting the advice here in this section.

The last thing you want to do before you kick off the actual event is make sure that your library and/or your venue (preferably both) send out one last round of advance publicity. Although there are definitely trivia diehards out there who will set their schedule around yours as soon as you tell them the date of the next event, for most people something like pub trivia is going to be a spur-of-the-moment decision, so be sure to get that extra message out either the night before or the day of the event. It's not a bad idea to send a reminder to your library's general e-mail for staff and volunteers, as although you and your staff may have spent a lot of time and energy focusing on making this event successful, it may simply not be on other people's radar, so don't be afraid it put it there.

This is where you should encourage your venue to do the same, as while it's likely you'll have some overlap in your distribution circles, they are much more likely to have reach beyond those who subscribe to your traditional library activity event feeds. Does the venue have their own Facebook page? If nothing else, make sure they either post something about your event there (and any food or drink specials you may have come up with for the night), or at the very least have them share any post you make on your own Facebook page for the trivia event. Hopefully they will realize that any publicity benefits them as much as it does you, but if the venue is slow to respond or otherwise dragging their heels, don't be afraid to push them (gently, albeit firmly) on this point.

You also want to check in with any trivia groups you are in contact with in Meetup, Facebook Groups, or whatever other platform they may be using to make sure that their plans haven't changed at the last minute. Since these groups often follow a circuit of trivia events at multiple venues, it's not unusual for some or all of the group to decide to go to a different bar or restaurant—perhaps it's someone's birthday or a holiday party or maybe there's a special on wings that night at the other venue. While this is of course not the kind of news you'd like to receive at the last second, if your trivia group(s) represent a significant portion of your event attendance, you may want to consider scaling back or even postponing your own event. Better to reschedule for a better date than to go to significant effort and not even be able to field enough teams for a proper trivia challenge.

◎ Running the Show: Setting Up at Your Venue

A good rule of thumb is to try and arrive at least thirty minutes before you expect your guests to show up. Get there any later and you'll be rushed to both set up your event and sign up your teams, but get there any sooner and you run the risk of your hosts not knowing quite what to do with you yet. Bear in mind that your venue is trying to turn tables, so if you and your staff get there early, do your best to stay out of their way until they have the space, time, and staff for you. Find out who your liaison from the venue is going to be for the night and be sure to communicate any needs swiftly through them rather than trying to flag other people down willy-nilly. Again, try to respect your venue's staff and their time as much as possible!

On the night/day of the event, you want to have enough of your own staff on hand so as to make sure everything runs smoothly, accounting for the following tasks:

1. Greeter and team signup. Make sure you designate someone with greeting people as they arrive at the venue. Are they here for trivia night? If so, let's get them signed up as a team. Did they not know it was trivia night? Well, they are welcome to join! If your venue has placed you in an area separate from the main bar, they could also make a couple of circuits through that area and let people know that pub trivia is about to start. A good greeter will manage to add a team or two by force of personality, so try to find someone outgoing on your staff to take the lead on this role.

2. Host/emcee. The host/emcee is responsible for communicating between the pub trivia staff and your attendees. They will read the rules and regulations for the evening's competition, tally and announce the scores in between rounds, and award the winning teams their prizes at the conclusion of the trivia event. They will also

adjudicate any on-the-spot rulings that need to take place (see the previous section on how to handle these in a consistent and professional manner).

3. Trivia question readers. Ideally the people reading the questions are the same people who wrote them: in other words, your library staff. Not only is it wonderful to see your staff connect so directly with the fruit of their labors, but it's also an outreach opportunity for the community to see another side of their public service librarians, as well as a demonstration of the depth and breadth of their knowledge. While it is acceptable for the host/emcee to read the trivia questions if the authors themselves either cannot be present or are too shy to read them themselves, featuring multiple voices for the event breaks up the monotony and saves the poor emcee's voice for the evening!

4. Question and answer sheet distributors/collectors. These staff will make sure every team has their answer sheets for each round of play, as well as distribute question sheets each round after all of the questions have been read. Whether you want them to collect the answer sheets as well depends on how competitive your teams are about turning in their answers first (see the section on rules and bonus points for encouraging this kind of competition!). If you are not offering bonus points for completing the answer sheet first, then they can roam the venue floor and collect them as people finish them, but if you are awarding bonus points for being first, you may want to designate one particular staff member as the official collector, so that each team knows where to run if they want to beat the others for that all-important extra point.

5. Graders. How many graders you will need is going to depend on how many teams you have. From personal anecdotal experience, we found that one grader could handle a maximum of ten teams, although your own experience may vary. At any rate, it is important to earmark as many staff members as needed to be able to grade all of the answer sheets and tabulate the scores before the trivia question readers finish revealing all of the correct answers for that round, as you avoid any additional delay time in between rounds.

Note that it is possible for people to play multiple roles here—for example, the greeter could easily be the emcee/host and as many people as you need could assist as a grader. Knowing who will be doing what in advance of starting the event, however, is an excellent way of ensuring that your pub quiz will run as smoothly as possible.

As far as format is concerned, we have discussed in a previous section about the various competition formats you can use for an event of this nature. Since what format you choose and how you choose to run it are both things that are entirely up to you, I'll take this opportunity instead to reinforce what should be your guiding principles for ensuring a good event:

- Planning. If you've come this far in the chapter, congratulations, for you have planned this event as much as you could possibly plan for any library event. Not only is the planning process good in and of itself, but good planning puts you on nimble footing when dealing with things that you didn't or couldn't plan for.
- Participation. The more people who are involved in putting on an event such as this, the more ownership there is among your staff and stakeholders, and the more energy and enthusiasm there is overall at the venue. If one person is carrying the show all by him- or herself, that's something an audience will notice; conversely

if everyone on your library staff is involved with executing the event and actively participating in one or more of the various roles as outlined above, your attendees will definitely notice that as well.

- (P)fun. Yes, the P is silent! Events like pub trivia are supposed to be fun. As soon as they start to seem like a chore, either in the planning process or in the implementation, then you need to re-evaluate what you're doing and why you're doing it ASAP. Don't be afraid to smile, crack a joke, and/or laugh if things don't go entirely as planned—your patrons have come because they have faith in your library's ability to deliver a quality experience and will always be your best cheerleaders if you let them. Never be afraid to have fun. By doing so you are giving permission to your staff to have fun as well, and a staff who has fun on the job is the envy of any workplace.

Evaluation and Assessment

We covered how to evaluate and assess your library gaming programming as a whole in chapter 5, but as the pub quiz is such a perfect example of an event that you should be constantly tweaking and improving with each successive round, it is probably worthwhile to take a closer look at how the evaluation/assessment cycle directly impacted one particular instance of this event. For this closer look we will examine how the Westport Library modified the rules, format, and even the publicity for their pub trivia night over the course of its inaugural round.

The Questions Are Too Hard!/
The Hard Questions Are Why We Prefer Your Trivia!

One of the first things that was brought to our attention, through face-to-face feedback after each event, from second-hand remarks made to the hosts or to other library staff, and from comments made on social media, was that our questions were "too hard" and that this was off-putting for casual trivia players. To be fair, when we started working on our first couple of rounds of pub trivia, our reference staff took an almost perverse pleasure in crafting difficult questions, so while this criticism was not unsurprising, how to deal with it productively was something that gave us pause. This was especially so based on other feedback we had received from members of the trivia Meetup, who said that what made our event so special when compared to other generic pub trivia events was the fact that our questions were so painstakingly researched and that the intellectual rigor required to answer them made for a more competitive and interesting game overall.

How were we possibly going to reconcile these two groups with one another, especially since the owner of our venue was squarely in the "too hard" camp and wanted to see us take some concrete steps to address it if we wanted to continue with his establishment as our venue? One clever way to make impossible questions less so is to switch them from open-entry answers to true or false or multiple choice format. Although the question in question is still diabolical, giving players a chance to get the correct answer, even if it's by guessing, kept them invested in the game when otherwise they would have simply tuned out as their brains collectively tilted. Another solution was to incorporate difficult questions into rounds with "beginner-friendly" themes. One of the things our staff did at the outset was dedicate each round of questions to a certain heading of the Dewey Decimal System: the 000s, the 100s, the 200s, and so on. While this was fun from a library perspective, the gimmick ran a little thin with our audiences, especially when we reached subject areas like religion in the 200s. While we would occasionally refer back to this schema, we ended up interspersing it with rounds dedicated to sports, pop culture, or current events, with additional holiday-themed rounds during Halloween and Christmas.

Incorporating Different Kinds of Challenges

Another criticism was that the play was, well, dull. Let's face it, at the end of a long workday and who knows how much time sitting in traffic, an event that was simply four rounds of the same format repeated may not be the most exciting thing in the world, especially if one team dominated the game early on. This is something we tried to address with the incorporation of a wager round into the format, where teams could bet some, all, or none of their accumulated points on getting the next question right. Although incorporating this wager round did help teams in the bottom third of the points tally feel like they were still in the game somewhat, I wonder if putting the wager round earlier on in the game—say between the second and third rounds—would have amplified this leveling effect and added a little more strategy into how much a given team would bet (which was almost always all of their points, with one hilarious exception where the front-running team did their math wrong and ended up in second place as a result!). Perhaps further tweaking is necessary in this regard.

Another feature we incorporated, albeit completely by accident, was the physical scramble out of everyone's seats in order to try and score the additional bonus point for being the first team to turn in their answer sheet. This was actually the direct result of one particular trivia night, where one team consistently tried to get their sheet in first with the result that all of the other teams caught on and tried to beat them. After this happy accidental discovery, we made sure to hype this aspect of the competition in future trivia nights, even going so far as to designate one staff member the "target" for handing in the answer slips.

Sponsors and Other Special Events

One last major tweak we introduced was allowing a local brewing company (Two Roads Brewing Company, based in Stratford, Connecticut) to sponsor our trivia nights. Staff from the brewery would bring free samples of their current offerings, branded swag, and other goodies—this in turn helped foster a positive image of Two Roads, a relatively new company to the area, as being interested not just in community but in relatively quirky events like pub trivia as well. This sponsorship led to a special tasting menu that our venue would offer as a supplement to their regular offerings, with little plates that complemented the beers being featured by our brewing sponsors. Certainly this required an extra level of cooperation for all three parties, but seeing that our sponsor brought an extra dimension of fun to the event, we all felt that it was worth it for this particular series of library gaming programming.

⊚ Conclusion: Community Outreach Made Fun

Pub quizzes are an easy way to showcase many different aspects of your library—your commitment to community, the research skills of your staff, and your institution's willingness to experiment and innovate in finding new ways to connect with patrons—while ensuring that everyone who attends has fun during the process. While we've only had the time in the space of this chapter to take a close look at one major workflow and several key variations, I heartily encourage you to look at other pub quiz operations (both in libraries and in the for-profit sector) and see what might work best for your own library and your own community. When planned and executed well, trivia nights can be enormously popular events with not only a wide cross-section of your library community but with your staff, your board, and other library stakeholders as well. Just make sure people keep having fun and let the event find its optimal form and format along the way!

⊚ Key Points

- Pub quizzes or library trivia events are a great way to combine the library gaming program with community outreach, as these programs can often reach demographics who might not otherwise come to the library.
- If your reference library staff is not currently involved in your gaming events, this is a great way to bring them on board.
- A lot of planning goes into sustaining a monthly trivia event, especially if you committed to writing all of your questions by hand—don't underestimate the amount of work required, and be sure your staff have enough time and resources allocated to do their best.
- There are many rules and best practices for these kinds of trivia events out there—don't be afraid to mix and match to see what works for your community and your library!

CHAPTER 11

How to Leverage Your MakerSpace to Help Bolster Your Library Gaming Program

IN THIS CHAPTER

▷ Just Add Synergy

▷ Print All the Meeples You Want: MakerSpaces as Gaming Support

▷ Hacking Fireball Island: Modding Your Games

▷ Go Large or Go Home

▷ Why Don't You Make Your Own Game?

▷ Emulators and Pinball Machines: The MakerSpace as Locus of Play

▷ Opening Up the Clubhouse

▷ The Missing Ingredient: Magic

▷ Emulation Is the Sincerest Form of Flattery

▷ Virtual Reality and Immersive Gaming Experiences

▷ No Winners or Losers . . . Yet

▷ Showing Off Your Virtual Goods

▷ From Cosplay to Printing Out Polyhedrals: MakerSpaces and Role-Playing Games

▷ Happy Little Orcs

▷ Why Buy 'Em When You Can Print 'Em?

▷ Arms, Armor, and Cosplay

▷ Conclusion: Gaming and Experiential Learning Go Hand in Hand

Westport MakerSpace staff Mike Altis (aka Breezy Dave) oversees the restoration of our pinball machine.

Just Add Synergy

SO FAR IN THIS BOOK we have explored how to implement gaming programming at your library in a variety of gaming styles and formats. At each step of the way, we saw opportunities for cooperating with your library's MakerSpace, if you have one. Even if you don't have a formal MakerSpace per se, you may nevertheless be able to reach out to your children's or teen librarian or someone else at your library who is responsible for coordinating your experiential learning programming. In this chapter, we will explore the various ways that gaming intersects with hands-on activities and the DIY (do it yourself) mindset and suggest how you can enlist your MakerSpace or experiential learning staff as allies in your quest to bring gaming programming to the library.

Print All the Meeples You Want: MakerSpaces as Gaming Support

One of the more interesting developments in the history of board gaming is in the restoration of damaged or missing game pieces. One of my colleagues told me that when he was a kid, he and his brother had received a copy of Fireball Island (natch) for Christmas back in the 1980s, which they played obsessively until, alas, they lost the jewel of Vul-Kar, arguably the most important component of the board game. After losing this piece, my colleague never played the game again until we had acquired a complete used copy from eBay! Who knows how many similar tales of gaming love and loss have played out over the years, for want of missing pieces? Sometimes it was possible to order replacement components, but the process was slow and cumbersome, with no guarantee of success—often the only recourse was to buy another copy of the game outright. As the spread of the Internet infiltrated the field of vintage and collectible toys, however, cheap and easy-to-find replacement parts quickly followed suit; and with the advent of 3-D printing, one doesn't even need to wait for the missing components to be shipped to you, as you are able to download the model and print out the game piece right there on the spot.

This has been nothing short of a godsend for gamers as a whole, but it is especially good news for libraries that lend board games out to their community. As one of the chief concerns about circulating games as part of a library's collection has always been "What do we do about damaged or missing components?" being able to replace most if not all game pieces in-house takes a lot of the pressure off the patron—who no longer has to worry about being on the hook for replacement costs—as well as the library, who can get the board game back into circulating condition with relative ease. Not only can missing pieces be 3-D printed, with models for most board games easily discoverable on Thingiverse or Shapeways, but missing cards can be downloaded, printed, and laminated; missing rulebooks can be accessed online as PDFs (or reprinted as well); and even entire game boards can be resurrected from high-resolution scans.

Your library's MakerSpace can usually help with all of these things, although whether to do so programmatically or on a case-by-case basis is a matter up for discussion between your staff and theirs. For example, if experiential learning staff are closely involved in your gaming program, perhaps your board games collection could circulate through the MakerSpace itself? Or maybe if you are weighing games on a gram scale upon return in order to flag returns with potentially missing pieces, perhaps this is when the items are referred to experiential learning staff for closer examination and triage, since this is the point at which the MakerSpace is likely to get involved in printing or crafting replacement components anyway.

◎ Hacking Fireball Island: Modding Your Games

Restoring missing pieces of course is the simplest and least imaginative use of your MakerSpace when it comes to board gaming, however. Why not use MakerSpace resources to modify existing board games or even help create new board games instead? Modifying board games is a time-honored tradition in the gaming hobby and can range from re-imagining and re-crafting the board and components to changing or adding to the rules to a game, which can involve designing new pieces or new cards or redesigning the game board from scratch. For example, to return to our perennial classic board game example Fireball Island, there are several existing "mods" or variant rules that add some complexity into the game—one of them involves taking the weapons from the board game Clue and strewing them around the island for players to pick up and use against one another or to confer other special powers onto the owner. Indeed, you see a lot of these board game mash-ups in the gaming mod community, and mashing up your own choice of board games can make for an interesting MakerSpace gaming activity for your community.

Modding can also just be about redesigning the components themselves. For example, take Catan, the board game formerly known as Settlers of Catan—given that the basic gameset consists of nineteen cardboard tiles depicting six different types of terrain, it is very easy to print each tile out on a 3-D printer or remake these tiles in a more durable medium such as wood, clay, or even metal. Your library MakerSpace may have a cutting tool such as a Carvey or a laser that could burn wooden pieces, or you may in fact have a kiln for firing clay to assist in the crafting portion with these materials. Of course some Catanians also choose to re-create the gameboard in less durable and more delicious ways, such as a series of cupcakes, cookies, slices of pizza, or even nachos and toppings instead of tiles! How they manage not to eat the game while they play it is a different problem altogether, but creating an edible version of a board game is a great library gaming activity for kids.

◎ Go Large or Go Home

Another way that board gamers have modded their games is to create giant or "life-sized" versions of popular games. While you may have seen this already with giant chess boards and similarly super-sized chess pieces—sometimes the pieces are replaced by actual people who may or may not be in costume as well—you may nevertheless be surprised to learn that gamers have done this with other board games as well, ranging from life-sized classic board games like Candy Land to a giant version of Jenga using two-by-four pieces of lumber and, yes, even oversized Catan as well. One of the more dramatic giant board games I've had the good fortune to play was life-sized King of Tokyo at GenCon 2017 in Indianapolis, where each of us had a giant cardboard cutout to represent our monster players in the game and we rolled armfuls of giant six-sided foam dice every time it was our turn.

There is so much going on here in the super-sizing of board games that your library MakerSpace can get involved with, from the creation of giant components and how to visualize the life-sized game board to the potential cosplay aspects of dressing up to play the part of your game pieces. For example, if you were to bring the life-sized King of Tokyo concept back to your library, you could combine it with a monster cosplay activity, helping kids create their own monster costumes that they could then wear for the gaming event instead of pushing around giant cardboard cut-outs.

◎ Why Don't You Make Your Own Game?

Why stop at modding games, however, when you can try your hand at making your own? Game jams—where participants get together to create an original game from scratch within the space of a day or a weekend—are becoming increasingly common as more and more people become interested in game design. Game jams can either be for video games or board games, so which kind of game jam you would want to host will depend on how technically inclined your MakerSpace or experiential learning staff is. If there's a critical mass of coding experience among facilitators, then you may want to consider trying to host a video game jam; even if you opt for a board game jam, however, you can have would-be video game designers create board game prototypes of their games.

If you've never hosted a game jam before, a great way to get started is to get your library involved in an existing event either on the local or larger scale. The Global Game Jam (globalgamejam.org), for example, which is held every January, is billed as the world's largest game jam event. It is truly a worldwide event, with seven hundred locations in ninety-five different countries creating more than seven thousand games around a central theme over a forty-eight-hour period in 2017. In order to host a location or jam site for an upcoming Global Game Jam, you would need to meet the following minimum requirements:

- At least one local official organizer to coordinate the event. The organizer must be a part of all e-mail correspondence, participate on Slack (for project management and communication), and oblige us with meeting all due dates.

- Secure physical space for the duration of the jam to comfortably seat participants. You can choose how small or large you want your event.
- Reliable Internet access (either wired or wireless) for all participants.
- Compliance to all Global Game Jam and local regulations with regard to hosting the event.
- Site hosts can choose to run public or invite-only events.

In addition to the above requirements, the following items are also strongly recommended for Global Game Jam locations:

- Access to all space and computing resources around the clock over the weekend of the Global Game Jam. You can still hold a jam if you do not have twenty-four-hour access to the space, but you should communicate the opening/closing hours to your participants well before the date.
- Local IT support in case of problems with computers or Internet connectivity.
- Coffee and beverages and easy access to food.
- Access to common game development tools and/or ability to download and install software. You might want to download this software onto machines or thumb-drives before the Global Game Jam date to ease the use of the networks at the beginning of the event. Also be aware of the resources many companies make available to jammers, listed here: globalgamejam.org/jammer-resources.
- Auditorium space to do an initial gathering on Friday and post-Jam presentation on Sunday of the jam.
- Security (safeguard against theft of belongings).

The Global Game Jam is platform-neutral, with participants encouraged to use whatever platform they are most comfortable working with. The above-mentioned link to Jammer Resources contains a great list for novice or first-time game developers, including special deals and free downloads for jam participants. Although the Global Game Jam is primarily about creating video games, participants may choose to create board games or other physical games instead, with tips and best practices in board game creation available here on the Global Game Jam wiki: archive.globalgamejam.org/wiki/board-games.

Whether you are participating in an event like the Global Game Jam or hosting your own game jam event, the format usually follows a similar pattern: the first half of the jam is devoted to working on your game, and the second is for playtesting and evaluating other people's games. One of the great features of a game jam is that not only do participants get a chance to create something, but they also get an opportunity to get feedback on their design, as well as help provide critical feedback to other creators' work as well. Game jams are usually not competitive in nature but reward innovation and collaboration among participants—the cycle of creative feedback and constructive criticism is part of that reward. That being said, Global Game Jam will feature games from previous jams that have been subsequently published, so it is an incentive for creators to follow through on their work even after the jam has ended.

Emulators and Pinball Machines: The MakerSpace as Locus of Play

In chapter 7 we touched upon how libraries have brought video arcade games and pinball machines into various library spaces. In the case of the Chattanooga Public Library, then-teen librarian Justin Hoenke added a Ms. Pac-Man machine to their newly renovated teen floor. Bringing the arcade game to this space wasn't just about the game:

> For us, it's not so much about the stuff we have but the connections and memories we make. The 2nd Floor is a community hub for ages 0-18, a place where kids, tweens, and teens in the community can come to learn, relax, have fun, connect, and more. Ms. Pac Man fits in pretty nicely with this theme. Since we got Ms. Pac Man, groups of teens have started to hang around the machine, doing their best to top one another in high score contests. There are eruptions of happiness every time a player pulls off an impressive move or evades one of those pesky ghosts. At the glorious age of 32, Ms. Pac Man is still creating connections and memories. It has finally found its perfect home in the library. (Hoenke 2013)

When we brought a broken pinball machine to the Westport Library MakerSpace, a similar kind of thing happened. Our MakerSpace, which until a recent library renovation was a giant metal framework shed that dominated a large portion of our Great Hall's first-floor footprint, never had any problems attracting the classic middle school/high school STEM demographic—in other words, twelve- to sixteen-year-old boys. Soon after the MakerSpace was erected in 2012 following a generous IMLA grant, the shed became a haven for this group, who could come in after school and play Minecraft, teach the community about 3-D printers, and just generally geek out in the company of their fellow nerds.

Opening Up the Clubhouse

The problem, of course, was that the space had been so successfully colonized by our preteen and teen boys that it felt somewhat unwelcoming to other library community demographics, who saw the MakerSpace as akin to a boys'-only clubhouse. One of my early charges upon arriving at Westport was to try to open up the MakerSpace to the rest of our community. We accomplished this through a series of programmatic changes, including opening up our focus on STEM to embrace more STEAM activities such as hands-on, low-tech craft activities such as sewing, sculpting, and other kinds of artistic expression. We also purchased a couple of high-end telescopes and partnered with the Westport Astronomical Association to offer evening stargazing sessions from our library's parking lot and assist in the construction of a neighborhood array of telescopes designed to facilitate the detection of asteroids and other small objects in space.

We also embraced gaming as a way to engage our experiential learning community, organizing several gaming events throughout the year, as well as more informal "pop-up" events where MakerSpace staff would gather to play various board games and encourage the community to join us—one such pop-up event was the addition of the pinball machine, which showed up with little fanfare one day in the middle of our MakerSpace. In retrospect a pinball machine was a perfect way to open up our little clubhouse, for it was just unobtrusive enough to remain in the background when it wasn't being actively worked on.

When our MakerSpace staff did start taking it apart in order to assess its state of disrepair and begin to restore it, however, it couldn't help but draw the attention from many passersby who may have previously written off the MakerSpace as a place where kids fiddle around with computers. Now here we had a vintage piece of gaming technology on display for all to see on a regular weekly basis (we established "open clinic" hours when our MakerSpace staff member would work with our kids and other volunteers on the machine)—people started to poke their heads into the space and ask questions or just reminisce about having worked on similar machines and electronics in the past. While the kids still came to the MakerSpace in droves, they were joined by patrons several times their age who were delighted to share their memories and lend their expertise. We also noticed that, for whatever reason, the pinball machine drew a more gender-balanced crowd as well.

The Missing Ingredient: Magic

Not only was the pinball machine located in the MakerSpace, but it drew upon MakerSpace resources for its restoration. For example, missing bumpers were printed on our 3-D printers, and our staff and volunteers figured out how to emulate the 1970s-era electronics on a Raspberry Pi. Also, when we did finally get the machine to play somewhat reliably, there was the shared experience of playing a pinball machine. For some, this was an altogether new experience; for others, it was a chance to rekindle old memories playing pinball in days gone by. As far as being a gaming activity that engaged the entire library community, this ticked all of the boxes: it was hands-on; it drew all ages and a more favorable gender balance than other previous MakerSpace activities; it got the attention of our library regulars (mostly in a good way, although there were the inevitable complaints when people got a little too excited about playing the game!); it drew upon multiple Maker disciplines and offered up historical lessons in machinery, electronics, and gameplay in a different decade. But most of all, it was a lot of fun. Fixing the pinball machine was fun, playing with the pinball machine was fun, even just talking about the pinball machine was fun. Not only had we opened up our STEM clubhouse doors, but we did it in a way that kept people coming back in time and time again.

This is the magic that Justin was trying to describe in bringing an actual Ms. Pac-Man machine into his library: the magic of the arcade, which for decades in American culture was a locus of play. Even though that magic has been dispersed, fractured, and overtaken by technology that puts more gaming power in our smartphones than an entire 1980s-era arcade had in all of its hardware and electronic components combined, enough of it remains engrained in our cultural memory that it can still be evoked by the sound of Ms. Pac-Man eating a ghost or a pinball machine scoring an extra ball.

Emulation Is the Sincerest Form of Flattery

Not every library can get away with bringing an arcade game or pinball machine into their space—some libraries simply don't have the space for this kind of experimentation, potentially fun though it may be for the community. This is where you might want to consider a library arcade project using emulators instead. We have discussed in chapter 7 about how most console video games can be emulated on very simple modern electronics like a Raspberry Pi, making it an interesting coding project for your MakerSpace. Indeed, the "Tiny Arcade" concept of crafting an operating console arcade machine, only in miniature, is not only feasible, but you can actually purchase the components for them from most DIY electronic suppliers such as Adafruit, whose creative engineer Phillip Burgess published a "not-guide" about how to go about shrinking a MAME emulator down to the size of a console that could conceivably fit into a teacup (although he protests that the end result isn't that much fun, it sure looks like it from my perspective!).

Virtual Reality and Immersive Gaming Experiences

If there is any chance of replicating the magic of the arcade with future gaming technology, however, it will likely be with virtual reality. For years gamers lamented the state of VR gaming, which with the exception of a couple of noteworthy attempts—such as Nintendo's Virtual Boy and Sega VR—seemed to be ignored by major content developers who were uninterested in taking on the risk associated with bringing an untried technology to the public. Then Palmer Luckey, a seventeen-year-old kid living in Long Beach, California, decided to jumpstart the development of virtual reality by creating his own prototype viewer, the Oculus Rift, in his parents' garage, and the industry has been scrambling to deliver on the promise of VR to the public ever since.

Presently there are three major "flavors" of console or computer-based virtual reality available to the general public: the Oculus Rift, Luckey's brainchild, now the intellectual property of Facebook, who bought Oculus VR in 2014 for $3 billion (Palmer Luckey left Facebook in 2017 after being demoted for secretly funding a series of viral pro-Trump campaign ads during the 2016 presidential election); the HTC Vive, which is a Valve product; and PlayStation VR, produced by Sony for use with the PlayStation 4 console. Microsoft's virtual/augmented reality headset (Microsoft is calling it "mixed reality"), the Hololens, is currently being sold to developers and should be available for consumer release in the near future. For mobile phones there is Google Cardboard, which is an open VR platform for virtually all smartphones, as well as Samsung's Gear VR, Google's Daydream View, and even a blast from the past in Mattel's View-Master, which takes the classic slide viewer from the 1960s and 1970s and reimagines it as a virtual reality headset.

No Winners or Losers . . . Yet

It would be unbelievably premature to declare one of these particular virtual reality platforms to be the winner in a race that has truly only just begun. Also, given the not-insignificant expenses required to get off the ground with VR, it feels somewhat disingenuous to recommend one platform over another when necessity may dictate which solution any given library may opt for, if they even have the luxury of choosing one platform over another. Instead, let us look at each of the present VR platforms and see what the relative advantages and disadvantages are, so that if you do find yourself with a sufficient enough budget to make a choice, you are able to make the most informed choice possible at the moment:

- Oculus Rift: The granddaddy of VR headsets has made recent gains over its high-end competition the HTC Vive and the PlayStation VR, thanks no doubt to the bottomless development checkbook provided by new owner Facebook. Whereas the original Oculus Rift kept you relatively immobile, the new Oculus headset allows about half as much freedom of motion as the HTC Vive, and its catalog of

Oculus-compatible games rivals both Valve's offerings and those for the PlayStation VR.

- HTC Vive: Valve's VR headset stole a lot of Oculus Rift's thunder when it first debuted, as it not only provides a quality immersive 3-D experience, but it also permits users to interact with an entire room of space, as opposed to the original Oculus Rift, which was basically a sit-down experience. The Vive still has the largest "room scale" virtual space, and although its game offerings feel more like proofs of concept and minigames, they do include the amazing program Tilt Brush, where you are able to create and interact with art in three dimensions.

- PlayStation VR: Thus far the only console-based VR platform, PlayStation VR has the distinct advantage of having its support built right into the hardware, making it a lot easier to set up than either the Oculus Rift or the Vive. Also, whereas the Oculus and the Vive both require a relatively high-end PC in order to run their VR platforms, the PlayStation VR runs on the PS4 console. The quality of the VR might not be as immersive as the Oculus Rift or the HTC Vive and your range of motion is definitely restricted to either sitting or standing, but the catalog of games for PlayStation VR is already impressive and growing quickly, including such big-name franchises as Resident Evil.

- Google Cardboard and other mobile VR viewers: If the PlayStation VR represents the "entry-level" VR experience for computers/consoles, then Google Cardboard is an even quicker and dirtier way to experience virtual reality. Making its first appearance at the Google I/O 2014 developers conference, Cardboard allows people to use their smartphones as VR headsets by assembling the viewer out of cardboard and plastic lenses and placing their phones inside the origami contraption. In fact Google Cardboard is the kissing cousin of the stereoscope, that nineteenth-century invention that used a split field of vision and specialized photography to create the illusion of three-dimensional images. Since its launch the Cardboard viewer has gone through several iterations and has myriad competing designs available from third-party suppliers, including the aforementioned View-Master. Google also has a next-generation smartphone VR headset called Daydream View, which is meant to compete with the high-end Samsung Gear VR; both of these headsets come with a hand-held controller, making it easier to navigate the phone-based VR environment.

Showing Off Your Virtual Goods

At the moment the sheer novelty of any of these products is such that simply featuring them in an open-play format is usually more than enough to showcase them to your library community. As for any kind of technology "petting zoo," you'll want to make sure you have enough hardware to meet your patrons' demand or, failing that, fairly strict time limits on how long any one person can use the platform(s). Since virtual reality can sometimes result in motion sickness or other similar side effects, it is extremely important to have your patrons sign a waiver before using one of the dedicated VR headsets—in the case of Google Cardboard viewers, which are not physically worn but are held up to your face instead, you can be the best judge of whether a waiver is called for in such an instance. The hand-held VR viewers are also excellent substitutes for the worn headsets, as each has its own recommended minimum age for use, whereas Google Cardboard and a hand-held viewer can be used by any age without risk (in fact, one my favorite memories is watching my then two-year old son peer through a View-Master VR viewing device to peer at fish in a virtual aquarium!). Bear in mind, however, that your Cardboard viewers require smartphones, which require both data and power in order to run, so you should make sure to have a couple of backup phones ready on hand.

As for games and programs to feature, here is a short list of some of the best VR offerings available at the time of writing this chapter:

1. Resident Evil 7 (PlayStation VR). As mentioned before in this chapter, this takes a beloved horror game franchise and amps up the horror factor by making it a first-person virtual reality experience.
2. ADR1FT (Oculus Rift). Basically the plot of the film *Gravity* in video game form. If you're not already having a claustrophobic panic attack, then this game may be right up your alley.
3. Tilt Brush (HTC Vive). Not a game, technically, but still the most breathtaking way to show off the capabilities of the HTC Vive by creating art in three dimensions with paint brushes that can glow and even pulsate when you paint with them. The first time you walk around and through something that you've drawn that's just hanging in midair is the first time you've witnessed the true future potential of virtual reality.
4. *Star Trek*: Bridge Crew (PlayStation VR, Oculus Rift, and HTC Vive). If it's always been your dream to serve aboard the Starship *Enterprise*, well, you're finally about to get your chance in this multiplayer cooperative game where players work together as part of a starship's bridge crew.
5. Keep Talking and Nobody Explodes (PlayStation VR, Oculus Rift, and HTC Vive). This is an intriguing concept: one player must disarm a bomb, while the other players tell that player how to defuse the bomb by reading the manual in-game.

As for Google Cardboard offerings, here are a few that are guaranteed to impress first-time viewers at a VR technology petting zoo:

- Titans of Space. A VR tour of our Solar System, complete with narration and jaw-dropping close-ups of our celestial neighbors.
- Proton Pulse. Remember the classic arcade game Breakout? Well, now imagine playing it in 3-D with your face. You can almost feel the ball sting when it hits!
- Tuscany Dive. Although there are myriad other virtual simulations out there for the Cardboard viewer, Tuscany Dive is one of the originals, and as far as demonstrating the proof of concept of virtual reality, it is still one of the best. Basically you use the viewer to walk around and inside a house in Tuscany—a simple premise that is nonetheless extremely rewarding. I still remember running a Google Cardboard workshop where an elderly lady was using this app and couldn't stop laughing!
- Sisters. If Tuscany Dive is my go-to Cardboard app for adults, then Sisters is my old standby for preteens and teens. A short, creepy "game" involving a stormy night in the living room of a creaky old house, you play by looking around and noticing the subtle changes in your environment until you realize a moment too late what's going on. What can I say? The kids love it!

◎ From Cosplay to Printing Out Polyhedrals: MakerSpaces and Role-Playing Games

In this chapter we've covered a wide swath of possibilities where your library gaming programming can fruitfully intersect with your MakerSpace's activities in the realm of experiential learning, from board games to video games and even virtual reality. Let us close this chapter out by examining how you can work with your MakerSpace in supporting role-playing game activities at the library. As with board games, this can be done in myriad different ways, as role-playing draws upon so many diverse branches of experiential learning.

On the simplest and most tactile of levels, many RPGs use miniatures in order to depict where a party of adventurers are in relation to their surroundings and their foes, whether they are other human beings, monsters, or other kinds of natural or supernatural hazards. In this respect there is a significant level of overlap between RPGs and war games, which should not be surprising as we learned in chapter 9 that the former actually grew out of the latter. What it means for us is that whatever possibilities exist for miniature gaming activities in your MakerSpace can count for both role-playing games and war games, which is great since often these are two completely different demographics that you can bring in, say, for an open workshop on painting miniatures or creating fantasy terrain for a skirmish environment.

◎ Happy Little Orcs

As RPGs moved away from the tactical to embrace more of a "theater of the mind" approach to describing action, miniature painting, once almost a requirement for any role-player, fell into relative obscurity until more recent editions of Dungeons & Dragons brought back a renewed emphasis on miniatures. In war gaming circles on the other hand, such as the Warhammer 40k crowd, painting miniatures has never gone out of style, although new popular crossover wargames such as X-Wing have brought an influx of gamers into the hobby who don't know much about how to paint miniatures but would love to learn the fundamentals. Miniature painting or scenery design workshops are also great opportunities for outreach either to your friendly local game store, hobby shop, or local war gaming community, as you can try to enlist their expertise in exchange for paying for their supplies and giving them space in the library and some publicity for their store or organization.

Rather than tie painting miniatures to a particular war game or role-playing game, themed miniature painting events can often be successful instead—for example, painting Revolutionary War miniatures for the Fourth of July or painting *Star Wars* vehicles and miniatures to commemorate the release of another *Star Wars* movie (which is almost an annual occurrence nowadays!) can bring not only war gamers and RPG players but people simply interested in spending a relaxing afternoon painting happy little orcs at their local public library.

◎ Why Buy 'Em When You Can Print 'Em?

While there is quite the selection of miniatures available for purchase by war gamers and role players alike, both varieties of gamer are increasingly turning to 3-D printing in order to design their own miniature figures, vehicles, terrain, and other features or customize someone else's online design. Obviously this is where your MakerSpace could really shine in helping gamers locate these designs online and/or helping your community create their very own miniatures for their own gaming activities. Gamers could also learn how to create and print out customized dice, tokens, and other supplemental markers used as gaming accessories, either to replace existing missing components or create new ones. If you search for dice accessories on either Thingiverse or Shapeways, you'll find all manner of interesting designs, including elaborate die-rolling contraptions in the shape of siege towers or a dragon's head. Truly, one's imagination is the only limiting factor at play here, as it should be when dealing with role-playing games!

◎ Arms, Armor, and Cosplay

Why stop at helping gamers craft miniatures, however? Live-action role players, or LARPers, spend a great deal of time making their own weapons, armor, and equipment, all of which your library MakerSpace could potentially assist with by offering workshops on how to make medieval costumes and period arms and armor. LARPing is really just the gaming equivalent of cosplay, as it can potentially embrace any gaming genre from fantasy to *Star Wars* to cyberpunk to 1920s cops and robbers. Again, this is an outreach opportunity for you and your library, as there may already be one or more LARPing communities in your area either looking for more support or who are willing to share their expertise with your library gaming community. Period costuming and historical role-playing can open up entire worlds of experiential learning activities as well—as we said at the very beginning of this chapter, just add synergy.

◎ Conclusion: Gaming and Experiential Learning Go Hand in Hand

This chapter only represents the tip of the iceberg where potential collaboration between library gaming programming and your MakerSpace is concerned. In reality these are two dynamic, exciting areas of growth in the modern public library, so for every idea that I've covered here, there are easily ten that I've overlooked. If you haven't already brought together your gaming library staff with your MakerSpace staff, now is definitely the time to do so. Instead of telling them how to collaborate, let them show you instead as they find their own connections, their own synergies, and their own room for growth. Gaming at its core is a form of experiential learning, just as Making itself is a form of play. This is why I saved the chapter about library gaming programming and the MakerSpace until the end of this book, as due to its all-embracing nature, it seemed a fitting capstone to this exploration of gaming and libraries. Where you, your library staff, and your gaming community take it from here is entirely up to you, but I hope at the very least that I've given you a nice combination of practical advice and heartfelt inspiration to take those all-important next few steps.

◎ Key Points

- The MakerSpace is a natural ally for library gaming programming, as it is also focused on experiential learning.

- MakerSpaces can support library gaming by helping replace missing components, but they can also help the community modify existing games or even use them as the inspiration for creating entirely new games.
- Not only is the act of play social in nature, but certain forms of play are coded to specific kinds of spaces—bringing items from these spaces, such as arcades, also evokes the magic of these spaces.
- MakerSpaces are also best positioned to help mediate access to virtual reality, augmented reality, and "mixed" reality hardware, software, and (of course) games.

⦿ Reference

Hoenke, Justin. 2013. "#historyread and a Ms. Pac-Man Arcade Machine." *Read Watch Play* (blog), September 18. readwatchplay.wordpress.com/2013/09/18/historyread-and-a-ms-pac-man-arcade-machine/.

Bibliography

Leveling Up: Reading and Recommended Playing

The Dynamic Trio: Hoenke, Levine, and Nicholson

I F I WEREN'T ALREADY FRIENDS with Justin Hoenke, currently director at the Benson Memorial Library in Titusville, Pennsylvania, I would have very much liked to meet him and pick his brain over several beers. If you are not already familiar with Justin's work and his writings, I would point you in the direction of his own list of publications: justinthelibrarian.com/publications. From his article "The FUN Theory in Action," I will share the following:

> In my pursuit of a clearer path forward, I began reading up on all kinds of perspectives on education, from common core, to STEM and STEAM, homeschooling, unschooling, and everything in between. Now don't get me wrong; every perspective that I studied up on had benefits for kids, tweens, and teens. However, one of the big things that I found missing from each of these perspectives was a simple three letter word: FUN. Realizing that I may be onto something, I started to learn about how others incorporated fun into learning. My search led me to Volkswagen's FUN THEORY, a movement "dedicated to the thought that something as simple as fun is the easiest way to change people's behaviour [*sic*] for the better."

Thank you, Justin, for blazing the trail, for bringing Ms. Pac-Man to the library, and for putting the radical notion that libraries should be fun up front and center for all to see.

There are two histories of gaming in libraries—there is the history of gaming in the library as an institution, but there is also the history of how gaming and librarianship managed to come together in the first place as a topic of professional interest. For this latter history, we have Jenny Levine to thank in no small part. Now the executive director of the Library and Informational Technology Association (LITA), Jenny is not only a prolific writer on the subject of how to bring gaming into libraries (see her trilogy of library technology titles: *Gaming and Libraries: Intersection of Services*, *Gaming and*

Libraries: Broadening the Intersections, and *Gaming and Libraries: Learning Lessons from the Intersections*), but she was instrumental in having gaming recognized as a legitimate area of library service by the American Library Association by spearheading the creation of the Games and Gaming Round Table in 2011 (www.ala.org/rt/gamert) and establishing International Games Day @ Your Library (now International Games Week), which she ran primarily on her own for the first four years of its existence. When blogging was the primary method by which our kind communicated, Jenny was The Shifted Librarian (archived here: theshiftedlibrarian.com/archive), and for a brief spell, she was the number one Google result for the search term "librarian."

It almost goes without saying, however, that the undisputed scholarly expert on the subject of gaming in libraries is the aforementioned Scott Nicholson, professor of game design and development at Wilfrid Laurier University in Branford, Ontario, and the director of the Brantford Game Network game lab (BGNlab). Scott was formerly a tenured associate professor at the Syracuse University School of Information Studies, where for fifteen years he lectured and published extensively on the topics of gaming theory, game design, applied gaming, gamification, and of course the subject of gaming in libraries—the course he taught at Syracuse about gaming in libraries is available for free on YouTube as a thirty-video series (www.youtube.com/playlist?list=PLhyRBdPvc WK59kRYL5LMV_s2Sz00oL-ph), and you can find the full text of everything that he's published archived here: scottnicholson.com/pubs/index.html. In library science, we are often accustomed to standing on the shoulders of giants, but in this discipline, we are beholden to one giant's shoulders in particular for our magnificent views.

⦿ The Extended Library Gaming Community

Justin, Jenny, and Scott are my three major points of inspiration on the subject of gaming in libraries—I would also very much love to run a Dungeons & Dragons adventure with the three of them at a future ALA conference. But look closely at what they've written and whom they've influenced and you'll find myriad more connections to be made. We should also consider ourselves fortunate that we are still small enough a cohort that our ALA Games and Gaming Round Table website is still a fairly accurate and up-to-date clearinghouse on the topic of libraries and gaming in North America and beyond (www .ala.org/rt/gamert). I've mentioned more than once in this book the critical importance of sharing in our profession. Librarians only benefit when we get together and compare what we've been up to, as we can profit from one another's victories and try to avoid having to repeat someone else's failure if we aren't afraid to share these experiences, good or bad, with the rest of our colleagues. So if you do something amazing, write about it, blog about it, present about it at a library conference; this advice also holds if you try to do something amazing but somehow fall short of the mark. Let us learn from each other's successes and mistakes, so we can all be better librarians in the process.

⦿ These Are a Few of My Favorite Games

It seems really silly to write a book about gaming in libraries and not to give you a list of games to be inspired by. So in no particular order, here are five games which mean a lot to me—I hope some of them will mean a lot to you as well:

1. Catan, née Settlers of Catan. One of the first "Euro" games to make American landfall, Catan is considered to be a classic by some but merely a gateway game by others and something to be forgotten once its purpose has been served. I am squarely in the former category and still play it competitively every year at Gen Con in Indianapolis.

2. LEGO Star Wars, Episodes I–VI. Produced during the golden age of LEGO video game titles, the LEGO Star Wars games managed to capture the spirit of the original trilogy and the prequels without overburdening the game with puzzles or mechanics too difficult for a child to figure out. These were the first games that my daughter and I played together—she was just turning five years old and, aside from asking me to help her with the jumps, played her way with me through all six installments. Ironically, she remembers the games better than she remembers any of the movies!

3. Pandemic: Legacy. I briefly mentioned how I started playing Pandemic with some of my colleagues at work as a team-building exercise. We enjoyed it so much and seemed relatively good at beating the game, so we thought we'd tackle Pandemic: Legacy instead. And oh, what a journey it was! From victories to defeats, to sudden plot twists and opening up little boxes of new components, the game surprised the heck out of us and gave us an actual feeling of dread that we might not be able to save the world this time like we normally do. Try and play it if you haven't, as season 2 of Pandemic: Legacy is out now as well and you don't want to be spoiled for any of this.

4. Dungeons & Dragons. For me the D&D "edition wars" ended in 1989, when I first created an adventure for a home-brewed world of my own creation using the Second Edition D&D ruleset that I have been running successful campaigns in ever since, up to this present day with an adventuring group of old college friends who meet via Skype every other Wednesday night. But I've had a chance to play a little bit of every edition of Dungeons & Dragons and will happily join someone else's table to enjoy some escapist fantasy adventure no matter what edition they're using.

5. Fireball Island. Did you really expect anything else to be here? From discovering it for the first time with my childhood friends to rediscovering it with recent library colleagues, to borrow a term from Harry Potter, this game has been my Patronus with how it has inspired me to think about gaming in libraries. The fact that it's wicked good fun doesn't hurt, either.

Books are strange things, for although they are meant to inspire conversation and action, as the author you rarely get to see this fruit of your labor aside from an occasional review (hopefully it's a good one!) or a "well done" from family and friends upon the book's publication. As gaming in libraries is a topic that is very near and dear to me, however, I would very much like this not to be the end of our conversation. If you've found yourself to be inspired or challenged by anything you've read here, please feel free to contact me at tom.bruno@gmail.com and let's keep the conversation going. Also, if anyone is ever looking for someone to play Pandemic with, I'm your guy.

Index

Aberdeen Branch, Harford County Public Library, 7
Aces & Eights (game), 86
ALA Games and Gaming Round Table, 14, 15, 50
Andrew Carnegie Free Library & Music Hall, 52–53
anecdotal data, strategic use of, 39
Anne Arundel County Public Library, 71, 72
Apes Victorious (game), 85
Apocalypse World (game), 85
Arneson, Dave, 77
assessment, 37
Atari 2600, 60
augmented reality games, 67, 71, 72–73
Axis & Allies (game), 52

Baltimore County Library System, 71
benefits of gaming, developmental, 13
benefits of gaming, neurological, 12–13
benefits of gaming, social, 13
The Big Bang Theory, 78
Bluffton Library, 71
Blyberg, John, 64
board game check-in workflows, 29–31
board game clubs, 42
board games, 6–7, 41–53
Boot Hill (game), 86
borrowing games, 23
Bruno, Tom, 29
Bucks County Library System, 6

Call of Cthulhu (game), 82–83
Candyland (game), 116

Catan (game), 45, 115–116
Chainmail (game), 77
Champions (game), 89–90
Chattanooga Public Library, 56
Chess (game), 2, 3–4, 12
chess clubs, 2, 3–4
Chick, Jack, 76
Chill (game), 83
circulating board games, 6
Civil War re-enactment, 52–53
collaborative storytelling games, 85, 86–87
Community, 78
community concerns, addressing, 79
community-driven programming, 14–15, 43
computer gaming, 61
console vs. PC vs. mobile, 58
copyright, 60
cosplay, 116
critics, addressing, 14–15
crossword Puzzles, 5
cyberpunk role-playing games, 87
Cyberpunk 2020 (game), 87

D&D board games, 90–91
Darien Library, 64
data, how to leverage, 37
Day, Felicia, 49
DC Heroes (game), 90
dogfooding, 28, 43
Dogs in the Vineyard (game), 86
donations, 23

Dread (game), 84

Dungeons and Dragons (game), xi, 7–8, 13, 76–77, 77–79, 122–124

Dungeon World (game), 85

Durham Public Library, 8

emulation, 60, 119–120

escape rooms, 8

evaluation. *See* assessment

event planning, 36

experiential leaning, 14, 24, 56, 114–120

Facebook Groups, 42

failure, the importance of, 26

Fallout (game), 85–86

Fantasy Flight Games, 88

Fantasy role-playing games, 81–82

FASERIP system (game), 90

Father.IO (game), 72

Finger Lakes System, New York, 13

fix-up gaming activities, 57, 118–119

Fireball Island (game), ix, xiii, 114, 115

FLGS. *See* Friendly Local Game Store (FLGS)

Friendly Local Game Store (FLGS), 21, 42

fun in libraries, xiii, 17

Game Designers' Workshop, 88

Game Jam, 116–117

gamer culture, 17, 21

gamers advisory, 17

Gamewright, 20–21

gaming literacy, 29

gaming programming stakeholders, 35

Gamma World (game), 85

Geek & Sundry, 49

"getting paid to play games", 16–17, 44

Ghostbusters the role-playing game (game), 93

giant or life-sized games, 116

Global Game Jam, 116–117

Google Cardboard, 120

Google Daydream View, 120

gram scale, use for checking out/in boardgames, 31

grognard, 78

Gygax, Gary, 77

Hanks, Tom, 76

Hero Kids (game), 92

Hoenke, Justin, 7, 56, 117–118

horror role-playing games, 81–83

Hovious, Amanda, 68–69

HTC Vive, 120

Icons (game), 89

increased library usage and gaming, correlation of, 14

Infestation (game), 93

informal games collections, 27

Ingress (game), 70

International Games Day. *See* International Games Week

International Games Week, 50–51

International Tabletop Day, 49

items missing pieces, 29–30, 114–115

King of Tokyo (game), 116

"Know Thyself" (γνῶθι σεαυτόν), 25

Kult (game), 83

LAN parties, 62

LARPing, 124

"learn to play" events, 45

learning tool, 69

Legacy games, 45–47

"Let's Get Quizzical", 101–104

Levine, Jenny, 50

library as arcade, 56

Lilly Library, Indiana University at Bloomington, 5

Lipschulz, Dale, 13

Little Wizards (game), 92

livestreaming, 78

local businesses, 20–21

lost items, 29–30

Luckey, Palmer, 120

"μηδὲν ἄγαν" (Nothing in excess), 34

MakerSpace, 4, 14, 24, 31, 48–49, 51–52, 57, 71, 113–124, 114–124

MAME emulator, 120

Mario Kart (game), 60

Marvel Superheroes (game), 90

Mattel's View-Master, 120

Mazes and Monsters, 76

Mearls, Mike, 78

media literacy, 29

mediated games collections, 27

Meetup, 42, 78, 99

Mentor Public Library, 7, 70, 71

Microsoft Hololens, 120
Minecraft (game), 63–64
miniature painting, 52, 123–124
miniature 3-D printing, 52, 123–124
"modding" games and game rules, 85, 115
Mongoose Publishing, 88
moral improvement, gaming and, 5
moral panic, and role-playing games, 76–77
Mouse Guard (game), 92
Ms. Pac-Man (game), 56, 117–118
Mutant Future (game), 85
Mutants & Masterminds (game), 89

New York Public Library, 71
Niantic, 68
Nicholson, Scott, 2, 5–6, 50
Nintendo, 12, 59
Nintendo Switch, 59
non-circulating games collections, 26–27
No Thank You, Evil (game), 91–92

Oculus Rift, 120

Paizo Games, 88
Pandemic (game), xiii, 46
Pandemic Legacy (game), 46
Pathfinder (game), 78, 81–82
Perry Public Library, 72
pinball machine, 57, 118–119
PlayStation 4, 58–59
PlayStation VR, 58–59, 120
Pokemon costumes, make your own, 72
Pokemon GO, 67–73
Pokemon safari and Pokecrawls, 71
post-apocalyptic role-playing games, 85–87
"print and play" games, 24
programming, 33–34
publicity, 28
Public Library of Cincinnati and Hamilton County, 8
Public Library of Mount Vernon and Knox County, 72
pub quiz. See trivia night
puzzles, 5

qualitative data, 38
quiz night. See trivia night

Radakovich, Boyan, 49
recurring events, 36

retro gaming, 7, 56, 60
Risk: Legacy (game), 46
Roblox (game), 64–65
role-playing games, 76–93, 123–124
role-playing games for kids, 91–93
Roll20, 78

Samsung Gear VR, 120
Savage Worlds (game), 81
"Say yes or roll", 86–87
Schiavulli, Amanda, 13
science fiction role-playing games, 88
Second Life (game), 65
Settlers of Catan. See Catan (game)
Shadowrun (game), 87
sharing with colleagues, 26
shmups or "shoot-'em-ups", 62
Shortz, Will, 5
Sidewinder: Reloaded (game), 86
Snatch (game), 72
social media, 27, 42, 71, 78
space needs, 79, 98
staff community involvement, 43
staff training, xiii, 17, 29
Star Wars, 51, 88
Star Wars role-playing game (game), 88
Starfinder (game), 88
state of video games, current, 57–58
Steam, 61–62
STEM education, gaming and, 6
storytelling, xii
Stranger Things, 78, 84
study of games/gaming, xiv
Super Smash Bros. (game), 60
superhero role-playing games, 89

TableTop, 49
"The TableTop effect", 49
Tales from The Loop (game), 84
telescopes, 118
thematic planning, 34–35
thematic programming and outreach, 51–52, 71
themed game events, 45
Ticket to Ride (game), 45
Tiny Arcade, 119
tournaments, 45, 47–49
transmedia storytelling, 69
Traveller (game), 88

trivia night, 96
TSR, 77, 85, 86
Twilight Struggle (game), 52
Twitch, 78

unmediated games collections, 27
used games, 22

vendors, traditional library, 20
video games, 7, 55–65
violence in gaming, 62–63
virtual reality, 120
virtual reality, comparison of platforms, 120–121
virtual reality "Petting Zoo", 121–122

volunteers and staff assistance, 81
VR. *See* virtual reality

war gaming, 52–53
West End Games, 88
Westport Library, xiii, 5, 57, 70, 71, 72, 96, 101, 118
Wheaton, Wil, 49
Wii and Wii U, 58, 59
Wild West role-playing games, 86–87
Wizards of the Coast, 78, 85, 88
World of Darkness (game), 83–84

Xbox One, 59
X-Wing (game), 51

About the Author

Tom Bruno is adjunct assistant curator of access, delivery, and resource-sharing services at the New York University Division of Libraries. In his 2014 book, *Wearable Technology: From Smart Watches to Google Glass,* he explored how libraries can introduce new technologies and incorporate them into the patron experience, including gaming through both augmented and virtual reality.

Tom has a bachelor's degree from Boston University in ancient Greek and Latin and a master's degree in library and information science from Simmons College. In his previous position as director of knowledge curation and innovation at the Westport Library, he supported gaming at his library programmatically—from collection development for games to programming gaming events and promoting gaming as experiential learning in the Westport Library MakerSpace.

A lifelong gamer himself, Tom is an amateur game designer as well. He enjoys board gaming with his library colleagues, has played Catan at the competitive level, and has been running a continuous Dungeons & Dragons campaign since graduating high school in 1990. He is also a devotee of the 1986 cult-classic (and, alas, out-of-print) board game Fireball Island by Milton Bradley.